Crowning Glory

**An Experiment in Self-Discovery
Through Disguise**

Stacy
Harshman

First published in the United States of America
by Andarina Publishing

ISBN 10: 0-997-3688-1-0
ISBN 10: 978-0-9973688-1-9

Professional Photography by
Gosia Wieruszewska

Thanks to Agent Thorn for sticking by me. I want to thank Tim for his patience and understanding. I also want to thank my editor, Veronica Tuggle, for all her expertise and help to make this book better. And my family - thank you, thank you, thank you. I couldn't have done this without you.

Contents

Chapter I
The Color Scheme

The Idea:

At three in the morning, on eBay, I bought a long, red wig. The style was fittingly called "Showgirl," and I fell in love at first sight. I had not planned to shop for wigs and had never seriously thought of wearing one, but strange things happen when you can't sleep and have internet access. Fully awake and thrilled, I spent several more hours investigating. I knew wigs had been around at least since Cleopatra's time, but I was stunned to find out just how big a deal they are. There were so many and so many different kinds. The more I read and saw, the more covetous I became. My mind filled with dreamy images of long locks cascading down my back. I couldn't wait for my new hair to arrive.

To understand my excitement, you need to know that my hair has been my archenemy since seventh grade. There was never enough of it, and what I had was wimpy. It became the root of all my problems. *If only my hair were better*. As a child, I developed a theory about why my hair broke off: Billy goats appeared at night and nibbled on it. It was the only reasonable explanation. Then, after taking eighth grade Biology class, I started hating my mitochondria for delivering faulty protein packets to my fingernails and follicles.

* * *

I went blonde at an early age. I can trace it back to my junior class picture. A bright color would make the most of what I had, I figured. Since then it's been everything from platinum and bobbed to long and yellow. Sometimes I liked it and others would compliment it, but the periods of utter hate always returned.

Maybe it's because I grew up riding my horse, and I loved his long, unruly mane. As we galloped through the fields, with my fists wrapped around clumps of it, I wished for a thick, head-tossing mane of my own. I pictured myself as a wild woman and the two of us as a speeding blur of hair. This fantasy would lead to bouts of bitterness.

* * *

I did have one fine, rare day when I was especially happy with my freshly cut hairdo. The smart, chin-length bob felt swingy and playful. A woman stopped me on the sidewalk and asked if I would be interested in modeling for a Prell shampoo commercial. She said that I had just the right hair type. She took my picture and promised to get back to me. My elation and vindication sent me running back to my hotel to tell someone. My mother howled with laughter, which I found a little bit annoying even though it was a shared joke that I hated my hair.

"Are you sure they didn't want you to be a hair double for the 'before' shots?"

I never heard from the Prell woman again.

* * *

The next week of painful waiting was relieved only when the UPS man finally rang my bell and handed me the box. Within a minute, I had "Showgirl" hair. BANG! I felt an instant flash of primal power churning deep within my belly. Long and radiating, thick, flame-throwing hair was at last mine. My transformation into a Fire Goddess was complete. I named myself "Kali."

That was my first impression in the private confines of my bathroom. I went public with my fiery self a couple hours later. It was August and damn hot outside, but that didn't stop me. Once out in the world, I was too giddy and agog to wonder if I looked stupid or lament about sweat pouring down my neck. Even my body held itself differently, proud and feline. I became attuned to my every movement and the weight and feel of the hair on my back.

Not five minutes outside my door, four fashion-challenged women, obvious tourists, gaped at me as I passed them by on my way to Soho.

"Oh look girls, she must be somebody." They all nodded their heads and beamed at me. I rewarded them for their recognition with a slight smile. *Yes, ladies, you are correct, I am.* Ooh, this was fun. As I walked along people stared, pointed, and felt free to comment.

"Holy fuck, you have a lot of hair!"

"God bless that hair!"

"Aren't you hot with all that stuff hanging down your back?"

"Hey Red, wanna have my baby?"

A man in a suit actually fell to his knees before me on the sidewalk. He threw his briefcase to the side, raised his clasped hands, and entreated me, "Please take me home with you; I'll do whatever you want. Please…" He looked so astoundingly undignified I had to avert my eyes.

I stepped around him and carried on uptown to my vocal class. Upon my arrival, I was surprised to see the normally taciturn twin security guards together at the entrance desk.

Usually one brother sat in a catatonic daze up front, while the other kept an expressionless post at the back. Every week for two years, they had mumbled "Hi", and had maybe managed sad smiles, but today, it was clear that neither twin recognized me. As I waited for the elevator, they shocked me with their cheery banter, awkward flirting, and giggles. Giggles!

On my way out after the lesson, a UPS man offered me the package he was delivering as a gift, two young guys fought for the honor of opening a deli door for me, and one older dude looked back at the wrong moment and ran into a newspaper stand. What the hell was going on?

I can't say that this has happened to me before. I mean, yes, heads have been turned in the past thanks to my Amazonian stature (I'm five foot ten) and my hardy, German-stock bone structure, but never like this. People have called me striking and sexy, but I've also been informed, too recently for comfort, that I am no more than average. My own self-image fluctuates between supremely irresistible creature to horse-faced, jowly blob with bad skin. In the months prior to putting a wig on my head, I had felt decidedly horsey and received little to no attention. My real hair, dirty blonde and straight, falling below my shoulders was blah, too

Was it all because of my new locks? Did the sight of them alone send out a flaming, five-alarm mating call? The attention went to my head regardless of the reason, and I admit to engaging in gross narcissism. I couldn't really claim that it was "me" getting noticed though.

The more I wore the wig out in public, the more that little detail bothered me. Who was it that the people were reacting to? Did it count since I was wearing the wig? Was it only about my outward appearance, or did my bolstered confidence have something to do with it? If so, would it follow that the more revved and high on myself I got thanks to all the ogling, the more ogled I would be? The chain reaction would escalate into a frenzy of navel-gazing delusion. Which leads to the big question: Why did I crave being noticed enough to insist on becoming a "Showgirl" every day for the last two weeks straight in 100-degree heat?

Well, the truth is, beneath the vanity and fantasy, my wig wearing had more to do with survival. I often suffered crippling panic attacks when I went out into the world, but that changed when I walked into life as Kali. I could hide behind her. If anyone rejected me, it wasn't personal, although I could let the attention in as mine. And it made me feel alive.

I was aware of my folly, but I also saw it as a weird miracle. This head of hair let me be someone else. Someone stronger. It also helped me escape a hopeless stretch of depression and desperation that had left me terrified and furious.

* * *

For years, I had been struggling with my own mind. I went to private therapy and searched for the roots of my suffering. I danced out my anger in my home and drew pictures of my pain in group therapy. I did yoga. I read up on Buddhism, philosophy, the laws of universal attraction, and all sorts of new-age ways to think happy thoughts, but I kept sinking. My psychiatrist told me to wait it out, and we'd keep experimenting with medication. He was sure my depression would lift soon. "It always does." I felt desperate and wild.

"You want me to just *wait*? I can't stand one more second of this. It's been five months. Fix it. That's your job!"

* * *

I didn't have a job to give me some sense of being a productive human being. I wanted to get one, but just the idea freaked me out. I did force myself to put in an application at Barnes & Noble; they wouldn't have me. Before the depression, I had rehearsed and performed music in the city. Not being able to play out with my band killed me, but how could I perform when just being around people was tough to impossible?

So, I went to music classes, played the piano, did vocal exercises, tried to write, and spent the rest of the day fighting panic attacks. Even being with my boyfriend, Tim, didn't bring me much comfort anymore. His resentment about having to deal with my anxiety issues had finally started to show. When a panic attack struck while we went out together, he refused to leave with me; I had to go home and fend for myself. He couldn't and wouldn't stay home with me forever, nor would he forsake his nightlife for me.

I didn't blame him. His kindness, loyalty, and patience could never be matched, but picking your wailing girlfriend up off the floor for the 'nth time couldn't have been fun for him and must have gotten old.

My morning pep talks went something like this: *Ok, you're not actually going to kill yourself today, so do something!* I used this motivational speech to muster up the courage to get a volunteer job at a holistic, new-age learning center. That got me out of my house and head twice a week, proved to me that I actually wasn't worthless, and eased my terror of being around other people. I started to enjoy my new little social life. So, thanks to my ability to hold down the volunteer gig for over two months and the energy and pretend confidence I absorbed from spending time as my Kali alter ego, my mind felt freer to wander in lighter places.

* * *

About three weeks after my redhead debut, as I happened to walk under the Dave Letterman Show marquee in Midtown one afternoon, I marveled over all the craziness that had happened. Maybe it was because the hair is red. *Red is blood, fire, sex.* Or maybe it's just because it's long and a ton of hair. Would everything change if I were a blonde or brunette? I was sure that I would feel different. What if I got the same wig in different colors and tested it out? That would be funny, and I'd get to gorge on the attention that comes from being a spectacle! I could even set up an elaborate experiment and write about it. That would give me something to do full time, everyday. Imagine—a structure. A goal! I need this.

Just wearing a wig around and getting looked at would not save me forever. I could not fall back into depression. Maybe I could write a book on my experience. Could I really make a job out of this absurdity?

Then it hit me.

WHO FUCKING CARES? It would give me a reason not to kill myself for five weeks. *Do it. Worry about the rest later.* And besides, people do stupid human tricks.

By the time I got home, I had my scheme all worked out. Project code name: Crowning Glory.

First and foremost, Crowning Glory had to be done right. Something like this called for a ridiculously absurd plan and a heroic effort, or it would just be dumb. I wanted heroically dumb. And I wanted to throw myself into a melee of action every day and every night, so much and so crazy that I'd be flung smack into life, shock the hell out of my depression, and never give it a chance to catch back up. So, the scale would be grand, but since human behavior (mine included) is uncontrollable and largely insane, I needed to figure out an organized and objective way to observe and investigate. That meant I had to come up with a "controlled" experiment.

* * *

The Color Scheme

I couldn't pull this off alone. My reporting wouldn't be objective, and I couldn't nonchalantly stare at everyone who crossed my path to see if they looked at me. Besides, I wouldn't have any fun by myself. My goals were lofty. I wanted all sorts of data, including stare statistics and psychological observations. This called for another set of eyes and an ego separate from mine.

I needed to hire a spy.

That decision set off inner alarm bells. Could I be around someone for so long? I might lose it. People scared me. Then I stopped and listened to myself. *Jesus, I can't be this dead at such a young age, can I? I have to get a life! If I panic, I panic. I can always quit, but I have to try.*

Only slightly convinced by my rallying cry, I placed the following ad on Craig's List:

Need Female Assistant for "city field research."

I'm doing a very interesting and fun social experiment – 5 weeks, 6 days/wk. I'll be the subject of the experiment. I need you to follow me around and observe and record what happens daily, take photos—quick shots throughout day—organize and log data, be available to accompany me to bars, (just to observe, nothing risqué involved). Should be able to give fashion/makeup advice and having a flair for styling hair would be great, possibly do light research in the field of hair and attraction and sexuality. Must be relaxed, enthusiastic, down to earth, have good social observation skills and like working with another woman.

—neutrality is essential.

—Quirkiness/interesting point of view is appreciated

As fate would have it, the perfect accomplice answered my ad:

"I have research experience and a good bit of beauty and hair knowledge. I have published a pop-culture beauty book and ghostwritten sections of a book on fashion design for a celebrity author. My observation skills are excellent… Your idea is making me smile. I happen to be really obsessed with hair…"

Bonnie and I met at my apartment to discuss the project, and I quickly decided she would make an excellent co-conspirator. She was thirty-three like me, a native New Yorker, seemed smart and funny, was a total girly-girl, appeared to have it together, and thankfully, didn't seem to notice that I didn't. Great, except for the fact that I wasn't used to being around other humans, and this one was pretty and had a lot of blonde hair to boot. I'd just have to get over it.

"Wait, that's your real hair, right?" Bonnie asked.

"Yes, well the color isn't entirely real, but…"

"Oh, please. Who has 'real' hair color?"

"Want to see the wig?"

She nodded enthusiastically, so I ducked into the bathroom and arranged my red hair in front of the mirror, then shyly re-presented myself.

"Oooh! That looks very glamorous. I love it. But I have to say, I really like your real hair, too."

Spy hired. Step one accomplished.

* * *

My plan called for me to go undercover and live a week each in the life of a redhead, brunette, blonde, and black-tressed woman. My spy and I were to conduct each week's field research in the same places, on the same days but each time with me wearing a different colored, long flowing wig. The fifth and final week would act as the control; I would go out and about that week sans wig, wearing only the hair that grew from my own head.

In the name of pseudo-scientific integrity, I designed a schedule to be followed during the entire experiment. Unfortunately, due to my lack of a happening social life, I didn't know the city that well, so I went to Barnes & Noble and bought a bunch of Manhattan guidebooks, joined Zagat, and hit the Internet for some serious research. My goal was to include as many diverse settings and Manhattan neighborhoods as possible to find out if, say, Wall Street has a particular fetish for redheads, or Soho secretly hates blondes. We'd sip cocktails in posh uptown hotels, have power lunches with the big boys in Midtown, hop dive bars until early morning on the hip Lower East Side, loiter in countless cafes, and walk enough city streets to wear the heels on my boots down to nubbins. For the next five weeks, my plate would be full every day and every night, and hopefully, if I survived putting these two hundred plus hours under my belt, I could get a life out of the deal, too.

Moments of amazement kept sneaking up on me. My eyes widened and tingled. I realized I had something to look forward to.

* * *

The Wardrobe

Once I figured out where to go, I then had to decide on what to wear. All outfits would be black, so the hair would be the color focus. I also wanted to vary the style of outfits and amount of exposed flesh to get an idea of just how much the whole package mattered.

That's when I realized I had to get things started immediately. It had been a few weeks since I thought of the idea, and it was already the end of September. The still sweltering weather would not last. A sexy, cleavage-revealing dress is not quite the same under a winter coat! I panicked briefly, but decided it was a good thing. Momentum was key to keep me from chickening out.

* * *

Modus Operandi

Bonnie would accompany me at all times to observe
and document any and all attention coming my way as well
as take note of my changing moods and reactions to said
attention or lack thereof. One of her main jobs was to keep
track of and tally the daily "Stare Stats," i.e. how many and
what kinds of people stared at me. We thought this would
be a fun way to obtain "hard data," and use those numbers
to determine the hair color winner.

My job was to live the part (obviously) and document my
experience to compare the outside world of what happened
and the inside world of how I felt. My plan was coming
together.

Day: Monday
Outfit: Business skirt suit
First Outing: Lunchtime, Wall Street, Businessmen
Second Outing: Afternoon, West Village "street time",
tourists, dog-walkers, etc
Third Outing: "Unhappy" Hour, West Village, after-work
crowd

Day: Tuesday
Outfit: Casual pants
First Outing: Morning, Chinatown Walk through, resi-
dents and workers
Second Outing: Afternoon, SoHo Starbucks, Work at
Open Center
Third Outing: Night, SoHo bars and street time, the chic,
the pretentious, the occasional celebrity

Day: Wednesday
Outfit: Artistic flowy dress
First Outing: Lunch (power), Midtown, proper older la-
dies, business crowd
Second Outing: Afternoon, Upper West Side, Affluent

families, Columbia students, nannies, tourists
Third Outing: Late Night, Wild card w/ Steve, Tipsy-to-drunk fun lovers

Day: Thursday
Outfit: Velvet fitted dress
First Outing: Lunch, East Village, younger crowd, punks, hippies, random lunatics
Second Outing: Afternoon, Work at Open Center
Third Outing: Night, Meatpacking District bar scene, See & be-seen crowd, mingling singles, celebrities

Day: Friday
Outfit: Mod Squad mini-dress
Second Outing: Happy Hour, Uptown (posh), sugar daddies, old money set
Third Outing: Night, Midtown, post-frat boys, office workers, after-work crowd

Day: Saturday
Outfit: Daytime: casual sweats. Nightime: smut-girl leather
First Outing: Afternoon, Union Square, tourists, shoppers, mixed bag
Second Outing: Evening, Lower East Side, Hipsters, rockers, loud revelers
Third Outing: Late Night, Lower East Side, same crowd, now drunker.

At high noon on Monday, October 3, 2005, the Crowning Glory experiment went live!

Chapter II
Week One: The Redhead, "Kali Amsterdam"

Date: Monday, October 3rd

Fields of Research:

    Wall Street lunch, 12:00pm – 2:00pm

    West Village street time, 2:00pm – 5:00pm

    West Village happy hour, 5:00pm – approx 8:00pm

* * *

Please may Bonnie and I get along, and may I not act like a total freak, I prayed to myself. This was a huge, interpersonal deal for me, and we'd be in cahoots together for a hell of a lot of time. God only knew how I'd react.

At least she expected me to be crazy; I'd given that surprise away a few days before. We had been in Sephora, shopping for makeup for me to wear during the project, when my plan of acting normal got derailed.

"Um, I have to warn you; I don't do well in crowded places. There's too much stimulus, too much everything, and I get dizzy. So, could you please take charge and pick stuff out for me because I'm useless. Meanwhile, I'll try to keep from fleeing." That was merely a gateway confession.

Bonnie seemed to know what to do in a place like this. "We want to enhance your features," she said, "but probably we don't want to do anything too outstanding with makeup. The focus should be on the hair, right?"

As she took charge, dropping items into our little basket and guiding me through the checkout line, I nervously filled her in on my depression and overall delicate state. She took the news in stride, and we had a successful day of shopping.

I suited myself up in my business outfit, donned my red wig, and gave myself a pep talk. Once convinced I looked good, I headed down to Wall Street to meet Bonnie for lunch.

I was relieved we both knew I was a mess going into this, but I started to worry I'd told her way too much.

I felt all set and ready to go, but ten paces from the cab door, I realized my definition of business outfit didn't quite jive with the standard wardrobe for women working in the financial district. This left me crestfallen since just moments ago I'd congratulated myself for creating a look with just the right mix of edgy and professional savvy. Now I could see my blunders plainly. First off, sequins on the suit jacket lapel and shiny beading on the skirt (no matter how subtle and tasteful) were no-no's. Second, a knee-length, pleated skirt worn with black, heeled boots was frowned upon. Third, lots and lots of red hair, especially when worn long and loose, seemed to cast one into the category of floozy.

My co-conspirator and I met inside a huge, indoor public area near the Stock Exchange.

"Hi. You look great! I think the outfit works! And I don't think if I were an innocent passerby I'd suspect you were wearing a wig." Her greeting was friendly and not the least bit wary. And she was here!

"I look like a freak, but thanks!"

We were off to a good start.

Bonnie's later field notes corroborated my findings:

Wall Street lunch crowd was almost all dressed in gray. I noticed that though your outfit looked business-like to me, it did stand out within the actual business crowds. There were no women in all black, no boots, no beading. Most women seemed to have bobbed hair.

As I walked around, I garnered the amount of attention reserved for wayward aliens. The image of a strutting peacock trying to look serious and neutral by covering itself with a bit of pinstriped cloth popped into my mind.

* * *

The place was mostly empty, and I felt anxious to leave and find the "right" spots. We needed to find a high concentration of test subjects fast, but we didn't know where to go. I looked around, thinking strategically, and spotted a nice-looking, thirty-something businessman walking through the courtyard.

"Hi, I have a strange question, can you help me?"

He stopped and looked startled, but stammered agreement.

"We want to go to a place for lunch where there are a lot of people. You know, *real* Wall Street people – where we can observe and be seen. Preferably where there are a lot of *businessmen.*"

He ran a hand through his hair, breathed a long *whew,* and looked at me quizzically. "I know where you should go, just give me a second to think..." He closed his eyes and rubbed his eyebrows in concentration. "Ok, so you need a place where there are businessmen, men, and lots of them... OK, I got it! Ulysses Grill. You'll find what you want there, or anywhere in the Hanover Square area is good."

While we talked, he glanced at me often but didn't hold eye contact. He smiled, laughed softly, and looked down whenever our eyes met. It seemed he really wanted to do a good job and give me the best answer. Pearls of perspiration dotted his hairline, and I thought he'd break out into a full sweat at any moment.

I felt completely confident and in control of him. If I gave him a little smile here, and a little laugh there, then he'd be apt to give me anything. This cockiness had to spring from my disguise. If it weren't for the intense pressure I felt to get things started, I never would've stopped a man in mid-determined walk to ask a crazy question.

After he left, Bonnie reported her observations. "It was weird. The guy was a big hand-talker, but he only did it with his right hand. He kept his left hand shoved in his pocket the entire time."

Aha! He didn't want to wave around his wedding ring! Our very first baseless accusation!

We made our way to Hanover Square and left a trail of baffled businessmen behind. Men had stunned and well-looky-here reactions, but women didn't like the looks of me at all. They tossed snobby regards, made scoffing sounds and cattily offered comments like, "Oh God, look at that girl in that *black* outfit and that hair. *Please…*"

Ulysses turned out to be a dimly lit, darkly paneled restaurant. The potential exposure level wasn't good, and it wasn't overflowing with businessmen, so we chose a place next door. We sat at separate tables outside and acted as if we didn't know each other, so my accomplice could observe freely. Bonnie spied on foot traffic in one direction, and I covertly observed the other. We were proud of our first big stakeout move. We sat there for half an hour, and a fairly steady stream of business people walked by. I pretended to read my magazine, coyly sipped my coffee, and felt really silly.

34 noticeable stares. All men, mostly white, early twenties through sixties. Mostly suit types but a few construction workers were especially leering.

3 delivery blue-collar types stared more blatantly than others.

Of all these stares, 5 were over the top, long up and down looks.

Bonnie trailed a few paces behind me, stealthy and all keen-eyed like, as I roamed down the busy Stock Exchange Alley: a pedestrian-only street in front of the Stock Exchange. I bagged a lot of easy looks from Wall Street guys eating their lunch outside as well as some catcalls from city workers.

"I like your hairs!" a burly construction guy shouted. I loved the fact that he admired every one of them.

A young city maintenance worker yelled, "I LOVE the color of your hair! God Damn, I LOVE that red hair!" I'd never experienced such specific leering in my life.

I felt kind of stupid about all of this, though. No wonder I got looks and catcalls. I cat-walked down the street for Pete's sake. And Bonnie, God, I could only imagine what impressions she had of me. As I heard her footsteps, I imagined a steady rhythm of her thoughts zinging off my back: *narcissistic, delusional, egomaniac, in need of help.* I winced in embarrassment; I had hired her to tell me how many people stared at me! It all seemed so outrageous. I also fretted she wasn't catching all the looks. *Was she cheating me?* But at the same time, I worried she would quit. Maybe she'd come to the conclusion that no experiment existed, and it was all just some elaborate ploy to feed my sickness.

On top of being embarrassed by my self-absorption, I wasn't clear *which* self I was being absorbed by. On the one hand, I lived the part. I *was* Kali and caused all of this commotion, but on the other, saner hand, well, I knew I was acting insane. So, I chided and mocked myself as I flaunted about, gobbling up attention. With Bonnie observing me behave this way, I felt even more preposterous and exposed.

I was finding out that Bonnie's definition of a stare was much more strict than my own, and it really bugged me.

"Hey dude, I think your idea of a stare and mine are very,

very different," she said. "I don't count it unless it's obvious. Seconds have to pass. A glance doesn't cut it."

I protested and called her stingy, but she stuck to her guns. "Complain all you want, but I'm here to be objective, remember?"

So, the numbers reported here are hers, but if you want my version of the story, multiply the stare stats by at least five.

Leading the way without knowing where I was going worried me, so I stopped two good-looking, young men and asked them to recommend a good place for lunch. Sure, we'd just had lunch, but this would net a little man-man-woman interaction and maybe even a reconnaissance idea. While the three of us talked, one of the guys kept steady eye contact with me and acted overeager and smitten. The other made an exaggerated point of not looking at me and talking to the air on either side of my face. Bonnie stood quietly on the corner a few feet away from me. I wasn't sure if I should claim her or not. So I didn't.

We didn't follow up on their "out of the way" suggestion, so we went back to the area in front of the Stock Exchange and set ourselves up at separate tables again. To give an air of authenticity, we pretended to talk on our cell phones. Seated, my short skirt, boots, and sequins weren't on display, and that made me feel more legit as well.

An endless line of businessmen, with big name tags slapped on their lapels, walked past. I'd say two out of every three snapped their heads back to do a double take when they saw me. I wondered where they came from and if they'd ever seen anyone like me before. *Like me? Jesus! It's just a wig.* But part of me wouldn't give up the fantasy.

When Bonnie and I got up to leave, I exclaimed, "Wow! I really got a lot of attention. Those guys all looked at me!"

"Yeah dude. You're wearing a red wig, a sexy suit and we're surrounded by a sea of grey. Don't take it so personally."

Hmm. I didn't care for that answer.

We left the financial district at three and headed towards the West Village to log "street time." This job entailed walking around the winding, quaint residential streets, the touristy areas and the flamingly gay area for about three hours with a few outdoor café coffee stops thrown in along the way.

I took a random left turn and ran into a gaggle of middle school kids. As I walked past the line of them, their little heads whipped back in a domino effect. The girls rolled their eyes, made mocking faces, and did crazy hip swings. The boys snickered and punched each other. They pointed and hollered.

"Oh, man!"

"*Oh, shit!*"

"*Damn!*"

"*Look at her, man.*"

Bonnie described it as, "Precious the way all the little boys saw you and then went nuts hitting each other."

A chubby woman with lots of brown hair walked past and then called back over her shoulder with a ton of vigor, "I love that color of hair!"

Some poor dude got a punch in the gut from his girlfriend when she caught him looking. Three guys kneading dough at a corner pizza place stuck their heads out the window to say hi. And every redheaded woman we passed, about six or seven, gave me long, appraising looks. I'd say mysterious and conspiratorial exchanges between allies, even. It seemed now I was on the inside of a redhead sisterhood.

We spent most of the three hours lost and finally discovered ourselves traveling around in big, concentric squares. It's not easy to navigate in the West Village since it's off Manhattan's straightforward grid layout, and here all ways are winding. So, we'd stop at a café for coffee, try to get our bearings and then march on.

I'd been freaking out from the start, but now I began to panic in earnest. My stupid human trick wasn't working. Big, crazy things needed to happen or everything would flop!

"God, I feel like we should be doing something! We just keep walking and walking, and we have to figure out how to quit going around in squares."

"I know. It feels like we've been walking forever doing nothing."

Oh no! Bonnie agreed!

"Wait. We're supposed to be walking around forever doing nothing. We're logging street time. That's our job!" I remembered with a flash of hope.

"Oh, right. I forgot." Bonnie laughed. "We should loosen up, and get used to it."

I smiled, agreed, and thought, *not a chance.*

This aimless time expanded into a big hole, which I found myself filling with ominous chatter. I offered snippets of too much information here, and patches of ramblings there. The shock of jumping into the experiment and interacting with Bonnie wrenched information out of me. I was stricken with conversation convulsions. In fits and starts, out came my life drama.

"Last winter I was depressed and desperate for five months." I heard my own nervous laughter. "I'm not used to being around people; just going out gives me panic attacks … I'm sorry, I know I'm not making sense. Does my wig look ok…?"

I couldn't control or keep track of what I was saying. My voice of reason waved its arms frantically and shouted, "*WHOA, HEY! CRAZY TALK! STOP!*" but this only addled my spinning mind more. The dizziness invaded my body as well, and I expected to fully discombobulate any minute. I was embattled, overwhelmed, and not at all happy, but the sane me was always present. I knew I was out of control; I also knew I couldn't fix it right away. The only way I could get through the day without running away was by going with it. My circuits were overloaded. I tried to sort things out but had learned that if I insisted on controlling the craziness in my mind then I would face total shutdown. The experiment was my only emergency plan for my life, so I couldn't abort.

My thoughts raced, but my head felt thick and full of a heavy, spiraling disorientation. Panic spread and added a lightning charge of instability and alarm to the mix. More words poured out of my mouth.

Oddly, Bonnie listened without flinching this entire time. She asked a clarifying question or two in between my tangents and seemed genuinely interested rather than alarmed. I felt amazed and confused that she remained unflapped by my whacked-out behavior. Maybe it wasn't that bad? Maybe it was all in my imagination, I thought hopefully for a moment, but no way could that be it. In any case, her stillness in turn helped me even out a bit.

And thank God we were laughing along the way. (Or at least I think we were.)

* * *

The time to search for a good happy hour bar finally rolled around. Apparently, no one comes out to play in the West Village around five o'clock on Mondays. We had strolled into the unhappiest happy hour in city. Finally, we found a little bar, populated with a few people, called Café Noir.

We took our seats, and I started to take off my jacket, but then I felt it magically being lifted off my shoulders.

"A woman like you should never have to take her jacket off by herself." I thanked the male voice, but waited until it left before I turned around.

Two guys sat at the bar and openly appraised me. The voice belonged to a handsome man in his early thirties, with long, thick dreadlocks. His friend, who was at least ten years older, had a mix of hippie and Harley going for him. He had a dark, graying ponytail, a stubbly beard, and he looked gruff. Their scrutiny elicited in me an urgent need to check on my wig positioning, but because of the tight space, I knew I could not escape their attention if I went to the bathroom. I got up to go anyway and tried to slip past them, but the gruff one turned to me.

"Forget the fact that I have a fatal weakness for redheads, you, *you* are absolutely gorgeous. Really. I can't wrap my mind around it." Suddenly, the guy's hand reached up to my head, started patting around, and he cried, "ARE YOU WIGGING IT?"

I froze, terrified. He didn't stop patting my head, feeling for incriminating evidence, and I didn't know what to do. I managed a sheepish, "No, I'm not."

His expression remained serious and sinister, but he stopped patting, nodded, and concluded soberly, "Oh good, that's you inside. Cool. That's you."

Smiling, I excused myself and retreated to the bathroom. *Fuck! Did he just feel up my head and ask me if I was wigging it?!*

I studied myself in the mirror, looking for flaws and telltale signs. Now I couldn't decide how far up on my forehead the hairline should be. I scooted it down and then up, down and up a dozen times before I just gave up. Then, I patted my head, like the guy just did, and felt around for clues. I don't know how, but he had palpated just the right places, meaning the one or two where wig infrastructure couldn't be felt. Any other spot and you could feel the basket weave lining underneath. Or maybe he could tell and decided to be nice, but he didn't look the type. Jesus, this was the first night, what next?

As I examined myself obsessively, I realized just how personally threatened I felt if people suspected me as a wig-wearer. A blow to my wig equaled a direct knock to my self-worth. Shit! My newfound life was built upon the fantasy of identifying with this as my own hair and the persona as me. Now I had to go back out and face countless potential head patters! A panic attack brewed, but I'd made it this far, and I wasn't about to lose it now. So, I unplugged my brain and ordered myself to go drink and be a happy idiot for the rest of the night.

As soon as I sat down Bonnie whispered, "Did that dude just ask you if you were 'wigging it'? I almost died!"

"Yes, and I did die, but I can't think any more. I need to just sit, drink, and be stupid." We cracked up and laughed until it hurt.

A group of young, bohemian French guys crowded around the bar near us. I chose the guy with the gorgeous thicket of dark, curly hair to be my imaginary lover. Bonnie remarked that perhaps he was wearing a wig, too. That led me to picture his bounteous hair flying off his head in the middle of passionate lovemaking. Then I saw myself screaming and leaving. I'd be pissed and bereft if he pulled a hair trick on me. Dark, wavy locks stir something powerful inside me. Would I give the guy whose wig just fell off a chance to let his inner beauty shine and win me over? Probably not. But if my wig fell off first, he'd be an unfeeling cad if he didn't love me as much or more with my real, less bountiful hair.

As I walked home, I welcomed the crushing exhaustion.

* * *

Date: Tuesday, October 4th
Fields of Research:
    Chinatown to Soho morning walk, 11:30 am – noon
    Soho Starbucks/street time, noon – 2:00 pm
    Soho Dinner and Bar frequenting, 6:00 pm – 11:00 pm

* * *

New day, new start, no thinking, no chickening—GO! After giving myself marching orders, I took on my first assignment of the day by walking (sans Bonnie) from my place in Chinatown to Starbucks in Soho. I'd taken this route many a time whilst wearing the red wig before the experiment began, so I thought I knew more or less what to expect. For example, I observed that Chinese men and women didn't give a flying fig about me, and they remained focused on buying fish, fruit, and whatnot. So, I don't know why, but heaps of Asian heads turned to take a look now. Deliverymen whistled, hollered, and got up too close and personal as well. To appear occupied, I nervously sipped from my water bottle and drank it through my hair. Then I jerked it down and splashed water all over myself. Twice.

Maybe the increased attention had something to do with my dressy-casual project outfit. I'd always worn flowing skirts before, so maybe the change into fitted jeans and a tailored shirt made my butt a new and prominent focal point. I told Bonnie about it when we met up.

"Before, you always walked this route in the afternoon, so perhaps the angle of the morning sun made a difference. Maybe the rays hit you squarely on the head, and you went along blinding people." She went ahead into Starbucks to install herself for covert purposes while I waited outside.

Thanks a lot. She refused to entertain the notion that I got attention because I was pretty, let alone special. It hurt my feelings, made me mad, shook my faux foundations, called me out on my narcissism, and left me to deal with monstrous, internal tantrums. It's not as if I could complain: She'd just call me out on my immaturity.

I walked in past the table where Bonnie had settled with coffee and a muffin. As planned, we did not acknowledge each other. I set up my laptop at the large communal table in the very back and began acting "normal." Bonnie's job was to worry about what happened around me, although I couldn't help but notice one man checking me out in a very un-sly manner.

The guy was a dead ringer for a middle-aged Kermit the Frog. He was slight and thin with shoulder length, pale blond hair, wore little wire-framed glasses, and had a matching long, pale face. At one point, I stood next to him in the bathroom line, and he quickly struck up a conversation. Turns out he wrote for a living and spent a lot of time in cafés. That sparked us talking about epic Starbuck fights for plug-in rights.

"Oh man, I carry a nine-foot extension cord with me at all times in my laptop case, so I'm ready… yeah, my EX-WIFE," He chuckled and shook his head, "You know my *ex* used to call me Mary Poppins because of all the things I could pull out of my bag. There's no telling what you'll find…"

"Oh, I'm with ya, I carry around a ton of stuff, too..."

He quickly interrupted, "Oh, not me, I travel light."

Huh? He'd just confessed to being a Mary Poppins. *I've stunned him into stupidity with my hair!* I gloated inwardly as he disappeared into the bathroom.

After I returned to my table, two cute, young women joined the bathroom line near me. I typed away and innocently nibbled from my fruit and cheese plate. At first, their whispering was too muffled for eavesdropping, but their volume gradually went up.

"Look at her with all that hair. She thinks she's so great. And she's eating cheese! Eating that big hunk of cheese with her fingers. So disgusting. Look at her."

Really? Did I hear that? It sounded so stupid I thought I misunderstood, but I looked up and saw them glancing at me with disdain.

We left at 1:15 to log some Soho street time. Right off

the bat, an ex boyfriend of a good friend of mine strolled past us. He didn't recognize me at all. After that, I laughed too loud and too often, excitedly pointed out displays of attention that I considered *grand*, then had to summon the will to wipe the pout off my face and keep from kicking Bonnie when she didn't agree.

* * *

Bonnie and I met back up at six. We went for an early dinner in the area and made a plan for the rest of the night. Our quest boiled down to going to the busiest Soho bars we could find. In the meantime, my biggest challenge was not eating my hair. Strands kept getting stuck in my mouth every other time I took a bite of food. I'd try to subtly pull them out, but too often little chunks of food were fished out as well and then the particles just hung there on the line until I picked or flicked them off. Very disconcerting. Leaning back on my chair was also cause for concern because if I rose up or moved forward suddenly, my hair would get pinned, and my wig would be pulled backwards.

Scalps aren't supposed to move.

* * *

Our first bar stop was a slightly fancier, Soho version of a typical Irish Pub. It was large and dark with a dozen or so people, mostly guys, sitting in booths and drinking at the bar. The bartender immediately started chatting me up, but I actually didn't care. I wanted to go home, and I wanted him to shut up. All of the adrenaline spikes and crashes, mood swings and negotiations with my inner warring factions had me bedraggled. At the moment, I felt depressed, dumb-looking, hot – as in too warm – and weary. And I had no idea how to engage in breezy banter with Bonnie. This was killing me. But I wasn't a quitter, so I made myself chat with the bartender and order another drink since I had my hopes riding on the restorative powers of vodka to help me make it through the night. Maybe it'd even induce merriment.

When Bonnie went to the bathroom, I still wasn't happy, and I noticed her barstool had gone missing. I looked around, found the guy who stole it, and prepared to go get it back, but then Bonnie returned and informed me she never had one.

On my trip to the bathroom, some guy marched in front of me, opened the women's bathroom door, and ushered me in with a flourish saying, "For you my dear."

That made me livid for some reason. So, when I got back I ordered another drink and glanced at the clock. It was only seven. My feet hurt, and my wig had started slipping ever so slightly on my sweaty forehead. I felt ugly, and the night had just begun. *Buck up. Bonnie will think I'm being too big of a baby!*

We took off after finishing another round of vodka tonics. Merriment had not been achieved, but I felt better and walked around for a long time without complaining. During that half hour, Bonnie recorded stares from sixteen men and seven women, three of whom looked bitchy. I focused on navigating the cobblestone streets in the least painful way and silently telling anyone who looked at me in a non-reverent way to fuck off.

We had a hard time finding sceney places and ended the night at Café Tina, a tiny Italian wine and espresso bar. It was too little for much of anything to happen. This horrified me since it could mean the experiment was doomed to failure.

"Thank God we get along, or this would've been a disaster. Could you imagine how much it would suck if we had nothing to say to each other all day and just sat around bored and cranky?"

I'd just taken a sip of wine, but this made me laugh so hard that I spit it back out. "HA! Oh, so horrible! If we were sitting here after hating each other all day, staring in different directions and wishing the other didn't exist."

We both visibly shuddered and tried to shake the thought off.

"But you'd quit," I continued. "No way you'd stay."

"Oh yeah, totally. I'd be gone." Bonnie agreed, "But we're doing great. We get bored sometimes, but we're having fun, and we don't have any problem coming up with stuff to talk about."

OH MY GOD! I'd just been given a stay of execution! She didn't hate me! Well, not enough to quit anyway. What a huge relief. My body instantly let go of a million stress balls. Of course, I tried not to show it, but the thought that she might really like me made me feel like a giddy little girl.

We were slaphappy and laughed through our bottle of wine and then called it a night. Although, when I got home, I wrote in my journal:

Feel like less than death.
Wondering if I'm going to be tired of this very soon.

* * *

Date: Wednesday, October 5th
Fields of Research:

Midtown power business lunch, noon – 1:00pm

Midtown to Upper West Side street time, 1:00pm – 2:30pm

Upper West Side loitering, 2:30pm – 4:00pm

* * *

Interloping into a big business power lunch in Midtown was our first order of the day, but before we could go, I had to figure out where those things happened. So I Googled extensively and consulted Zagat to find a worthy place. The *21 Club* came out the winner. They'd been in business since 1929 and described themselves as:

Once a glamorous speakeasy, today '21' is one of the most celebrated restaurants in New York City... the watering hole of celebrities, captains of industry, world leaders and dignitaries of every order.

That sounded just right, so I made a reservation online for lunch in the legendary Bar Room.

An establishment like this probably frowned upon arriving fashionably late, so I arrived early and checked out ole *21* while I waited. Off to the side of the main entrance, a spiraling, iron stairwell led up to a large terrace. A dozen or so mini-statues of diminutive jockeys—outfitted in a colorful array of silks—lined the stairs and stood poised at the terrace railing. I decided this was strictly for show, and I wasn't supposed to go up there. This scene struck me as goofy looking and not very austere. In between trying to figure out what was up with the jockeys, I watched impeccably suited groups of men pass between the old-fashioned carriage lights, walk down the wide stairs, and enter *21*.

My "artistic dress" was long, billowy, and pretty. Even with its décolleté, I thought it was respectable, but I had a feeling that assessment would change. Then Bonnie arrived looking nice and neutral, which was a good thing, but I flinched with the knowledge that I'd be bearing any freak burden. Now I was nervous.

The maître d' flashed a sign of wide-eyed alarm when we announced ourselves, but he treated us graciously and led us to our table. As I followed him into the dining area, I was positive I looked ridiculous and that everyone staring at me agreed with that assessment, but for survival and pride reasons, my ego roared back and commanded me to hold my head high and believe people were admiring my striking presence.

It wasn't working.

I can't do this. God. I can't do this!

At that instant, autopilot took over, checked me out, and turned me into a character walking inside a movie. Everything was distant yet grotesquely exaggerated; the sound of my heels echoed in my ears, bloated faces crowded my vision, the maître d' raced ahead, but an eternity passed before we made it to our seats.

I steadied myself as I watched him pull out the table and motion for one of us to sit inside on the banquet. Bonnie slid in and I waited, but he didn't move the table back. That's when I noticed that the table did not have a chair on the outside.

"Please," he said, as he again signaled for me to sit next to Bonnie, "This is how we seat our guests here at 21."

Ok. *I don't like this!* But in I went.

We sat side by side on a large, red banquette that wrapped all around the room. We couldn't avoid looking out at everyone seated at the tables in the middle of the dining room as well as those seated on the unending banquette lining the wall opposite us. And vice versa. I turned to Bonnie, who appeared mortified, and eyed the space behind her back; I wanted to crawl in there.

Many of the men regarded us curiously, and I noticed many others made a point not to look in our direction. A touch of amusement and a you-silly-girls attitude towards our presence seemed to pervade the entire dining room. The last thing I wanted to do was look up from my plate. I felt bare-ass nekked, and my hair embarrassed me. Hot shame and anger shot through me at the very thought of being humiliated. I was surrounded by hostiles, deep in enemy territory.

"I'm embarrassed. I don't know what to do. I want to hide."

"Oh, we look like complete fools. This is horrifying." Bonnie whispered back.

When the food came, I was relieved to have something to focus on. My lemon had a hair net over it, and I admired the way it caught the seeds when I squeezed it onto my fish. This little discovery soothed me, and eating made me feel more legitimate. *See, I'm here for lunch, just like you.* The headwaiter treated us well, and our chief table server couldn't have been more formal and gracious. But it all felt weird to me. He virtually did everything for us, laying napkins on our laps, salt and peppering our food, and even went the extra mile for the guy sitting next to me by spooning ketchup onto his burger for him.

Finally, I thawed out and switched to fancying myself as some exotic, UN ambassador/model type who was at home anywhere, like Angelina Jolie.

At first, Bonnie and I only dared to whisper a few words to each other, but her spy notes reveal her thoughts:

This place was so classic and funny. Totally dark wood paneling with a ceiling decorated with toy airplanes, trucks, etc. We sort of looked/felt like hookers since we were the only young women in there. There were literally people there wearing bow ties. We could not have been more out of place.

When it came time for dessert, the waiter made an announcement to the entire room, and to us:

"Because you made the reservation online you each get a complimentary glass of champagne courtesy of *Club 21*." We accepted it, which made everything even funnier.

"Now I've switched from feeling like a hooker to just a dazzled, weirdo tourist," Bonnie whispered over her champagne flute.

I, on the other hand, kept on pretending to be Angelina. On the way out, a very old bartender gave me a commemorative pen and promised to give me another if I returned.

* * *

Logging street time in Midtown and then hanging out in the Upper West Side was scheduled for the rest of the day. We walked through boutique-lined avenues around the Fifty-Seventh Street area and made our way north. We ambled for thirty or so minutes, all the while my spy faithfully counted stares (about twenty).

Unsure of what to do next, we went into the Time Warner Center mall. To my delight, we happened upon a psychic fair put on by Court TV for their new psychic detective show. We hurried up to the second floor where sixty psychics, each perched at separate tall, round tables, were gathered in a roped off area. We joined the long line for a free reading.

Amongst the sixty, a couple of flamboyant women with long red hair were revealing secrets with each turn of their Tarot cards.

"You look like you should be one of them!"

"I know. And I've always wanted to be a gypsy!" The line moved slowly. Once again, I found myself telling Bonnie about some of the stranger aspects of being me.

Sure, everyone has at least some idea of what depression means, but could she understand the rest? I described how intense and weird the manic period could be for me.

"At some point I slipped into believing the unbelievable. That's the scary part. The change is imperceptible. Looking back on it, now that I'm not manic, I remember my mind being geared up; I was seeing signs, connecting lots of dots, and my thoughts were capable of leaping the universe in one single bound. My reason still existed, but I was being persuaded, tempted by this intoxicating, speeding mental state."

"What kinds of signs?"

"Oh, you know," I tried for a casual tone. "I was walking around the city, taking advice from the snake gods, that kind of thing."

"...The snake gods?"

Maybe I had finally hit her limit. I rushed to explain. I wanted her to see me as normal. "I knew better, I'd been there before. I should've started taking the meds that bring me down, but I wanted to ride the high just a little longer. It's like, who wants to turn off their super-powers? But then it slips past me. BAM. No transition. It's real, and I'm talking to snakes."

Bonnie nodded.

We were getting close to the head of the line, and I was relieved when she started to joke around.

"I wonder if your psychic will take one look at you and proclaim you lead a fiery, passionate life."

"Right, then we'll know for sure it's the hair! Well, unless the seer throws in some crashing and burning, depression and hell, madness and mania into my fate as well."

"That would be impressive but a little too freaky."

"I will freak if the psychic tells me one of my snake spirit friends says hi."

"Me too."

Finally, we were up next.

"Check on my wig positioning please. I can't have my own hair poking out while I'm sitting in front of my psychic. I'm paranoid as it is!"

"It looks fine, don't worry. Half of them are probably wearing wigs anyway!"

The woman who did my numerology reading looked suspiciously ordinary. She'd probably been a stay-at-home mom who did seamstress work on the side and had added psychic stuff once the kids got older. Although, she didn't seem the least bit bothered or swayed by my appearance, I didn't quite trust her. Nothing too surprising or shocking came up, but she did go on about elaborate, collaborative projects that were happening or coming in my near future and warned me not to lose myself.

While I waited for Bonnie's reading to finish, I caught an old, hairy man pretending to talk on his cell phone, so he could continue to hover near me. He never moved his mouth. Wow, I hoped we performed the cell phone trick more convincingly than that.

"Do you really think he was doing that so he could hang around?" I asked Bonnie when she rejoined me.

"Oh yeah, definitely. I do it when I see celebrities or whenever I want to gawk for an extended time. Everybody uses it."

On our way out, I noticed the Mandarin Oriental Hotel was across the street. I'd never been inside, but I'd fantasized about spending a deviant weekend with a mysterious lover in this urban, opium love den. *Mandarin Oriental.* I mean the name just beckoned taboo bliss.

"Ooh, can we go in? I want to see if it matches my love palace dreams!"

"I don't think sightseeing is on our experiment schedule today."

"It counts as research! Come on, *please.*"

As soon as we went in, I knew my instincts were correct. Everything about the place, from the lighting to the décor, called out for a dark torrid affair. Out of curiosity, we went up to check out the bar on the 35th floor. As we rode up in the elevator with an uptight looking, middle-aged woman, I gushed to Bonnie, "I want to have a steamy affair here, right now. I don't want to wait for someday! Oh, where's my dark, handsome sheik that jets in just to be in my arms at midnight?" I stamped my foot.

Upon my exclamatory foot stamp on the elevator floor, the uptight looking woman shot me a glaring look of disapproval and shook her head as she walked into the lobby.

"She's obviously here for business purposes."

"The only glitch in my plan is that I have no desire for my boyfriend to be present," I said. Our relationship had always been more of a comfort zone than a passionate affair.

"Yep, I can see how that could be a problem, but we've strayed from our mission. Let's go. We're not here to check out your fantasy locales." And Bonnie pushed me out the elevator door.

* * *

We spent the rest of the afternoon plopped down at a table in a large sidewalk seating area of a café on Broadway, near Lincoln Center. Our seat gave us a perfect pedestrian observation post while we sucked down more coffee, ate cake, and hoped to God all our walking cancelled out all our drinking and eating.

The area wasn't that busy, but a steady trickle of people walked by. Bonnie noted several wistful looks from women with "unfortunate hair." I sympathized. For most of my life, I'd looked longingly at women with Kali-like hair, and I had secretly or openly hated them. Now I indulged in feeling superior. *Poor dears, I used to be like you.*

I didn't realize just how much more air space my head occupied, though. Two older women, sitting behind us and engrossed in energetic discussions about theater, good-naturedly informed me, "You need to control that hair of yours, or you're going to have wine down your back."

Our workday ended at four-thirty. My therapist appointment was at five, and I needed to be another forty blocks uptown, so I took the subway since it'd be quicker than a cab.

I ran to make it onto a packed rush hour train, and as I pushed my way in, I suddenly felt myself being yanked backwards. Looking behind me, I saw what appeared to be a yard of red hair, stretched taut and stuck in between the closed subway doors. As I gaped in confused horror, the

doors re-opened slightly, and I freed myself. Trying not to image the ugly scene I just narrowly escaped, I made a stern note to self: DO NOT STAND TOO CLOSE TO THE CLOSING SUBWAY DOORS.

Now I was packed tightly against strangers who were more or less eye level with my forehead and had nothing better to do than gaze at my messed-up hairline. A plump and dowdy redheaded woman, standing less than three feet away from me, wouldn't stop staring. She had an obnoxious look on her face, and I wanted to harm her. Even though I felt ridiculous, I glared back and snarled until she looked away.

In the next instant, people started rushing off the train, and my hair was being tugged on from two different directions. Strands were snagged on a passing purse zipper on my left and wrapped around an incoming briefcase latch on my right. I yanked them out frantically and held onto my synthetic scalp as discreetly as I could.

In search of a safer place, I moved closer to the center of the car. Five teenage Latinas sat near me, giggling and whispering in Spanish. I feigned normalcy as I held onto the bar and tried to ignore them. But then I heard one of them say the word "*peluca*," which means "wig," amidst their snickering. Red alert!

The oldest and wickedest girl of the bunch looked up at me in a mean manner. She said, in Spanish, "What if I get up and act like I'm reaching for the railing and pretend to get my hand tangled in her hair and see what happens… dare me?"

"*Sí!*" The others howled. That was my cue to move.

Once above ground and amazed I'd avoided full disaster, I vowed I would never take the subway in rush hour again.

* * *

My therapist looked at me with her very concerned face. It read, *I don't approve; this is not emotionally healthy.* I've always hated this look. Now more than ever. The last thing I wanted was to be sitting opposite her, wearing a wig, and updating her on my project.

Last week, I had told her about the experiment and immediately felt the need to defend it. I had been convinced she thought I was only doing this to run away from my demons and that I was going about it in the worst way: by using my old addiction to attention from men to lift me up and away from myself. True, she had me there, but I had felt like screaming, *It's the only thing I have, the only thing that makes me feel alive, so don't you fucking dare take it away!* Instead, I had flopped around under her critical gaze, feeling convicted of betraying my higher self, and tried to justify the experiment's higher meaning.

"I'll be studying the overblown value society places on external trappings and how looks can equal power in the world…." I had been reaching.

Her semi-horrified, semi-incredulous expression hadn't changed, but she had responded by asking me to tell her more.

So, I had tried to explain my reasoning and come up with proof of spiritual merit as well as examples of why this project would be at all interesting to anyone besides me. "Well, and you know, everyone is interested in the mystery of sexual attraction, inner identity versus outward appearance, how others' perceptions affects individual self-esteem…and it's not like I'm a supermodel. I don't get tons of attention now, so if I put a wig on and poof, men go crazy over me, then there's definitely a change, and it's a believable and relatable experience."

"You're right. You're just an average woman putting a wig on, just like any woman off the street."

What?! Average?! She had kicked me in the gut! A violent storm of emotions erupted inside me as I sat there, mute and enraged. How could she? My feelings had been crushed, and I had started to panic because I wasn't pretty, and that led to all sorts of doom. But, if I had argued, all my higher meaning talk would have proven to be BS. I couldn't stand to hear anymore. That was it. FUCK YOU. Conversation over.

She'd attacked my ego, so I had closed up tighter than a mad clam, but she'd warmed up to my idea. Suddenly her tone changed. "You know, we always do something for more than one reason. There's the outward, stated one but then there's a deeper, personal layer. You're doing this because you need to learn something about yourself. This is good."

I was still reeling from the pain of being called average, so I didn't really take in her voice of approval for the project. It did make sense to me that I was doing this for many different reasons, some of which might actually be healing for me. I took some solace in that.

So now, a week later, I had no desire to tell her anything. I did want to talk about the extreme emotional rollercoaster I'd been on and how painfully hard it was to keep myself together, but I was afraid of what she'd say. At the heart of it, I did feel threatened and worthless if I thought a man didn't consider me desirable. The difference between getting even a fleeting, flirty glance and not getting noticed was heaven and hell. My fear, terror even, of not being "pretty" ran deep. And I'd just set myself up to go through this countless times a day. I'd been battered and needed help, but my fragile ego couldn't risk talking about it. We discussed trivial matters until my time was up and I could escape.

* * *

Date: Thursday, October 6th
Fields of research:
    East Village lunch, noon – 2:00pm
    Upper West Side/Columbus University area, dinner,
8:00pm
    Various Upper West Side bars, street time, 6:00pm –
11:00pm

* * *

Bonnie and I met up around noon in the East Village for lunch and street time.

Teenage attention seekers and freaky types hang around in this area, so odd hair, body art, and abundant piercings are common. I guessed it'd be hard work to get noticed here, and I was correct. No one really paid attention to me. I didn't like it.

From there, I went to the Open Center in Soho to work my afternoon volunteer shift. The Center is a well-established mecca for a variety of New Age, holistic-type offerings. My job entailed booking massages and energy work appointments in the Wellness Department.

I'd worked there for a few months before I discovered wigs, so I came into plenty of contact with everyone as the real me. Ever since I had started wearing the red one, the general manager often gazed at me with a beatific expression, smiling warmly. There wasn't any hint of recognition or surprise, just a warm smile. *He must be into me in some weird, holistic way*, I thought.

That day, the receptionist, laughing, called me over. "Girl, you're not going to believe this. Listen, you know Thomas, the general manager? Well, he thought you had cancer!"

"What! Why?"

"Well he told me, 'I thought, here's a young girl wearing

a wig; it can only be cancer.' So, every time he saw you, he focused on sending you light and healing energy. Bless him. I just told him about the experiment. He was surprised but said, 'Well, as long as she's well, I'm glad.'"

"Are you kidding me? I'm so embarrassed. And he knew it was a wig from the beginning? Oh God, I look stupid!"

"No, no honey, I told you I think you look great, and it really looks natural on you. And I love the color. Honest. Look, I have no idea how he knew, maybe he's into wigs or something, but you know what *is* weird; he didn't have any idea what you looked like or remember you at all before this. I even described what you looked like and told him you'd been here for months, but he said no, he had no idea who you were. But that was sweet of him to send you blessings…"

Yes, very sweet, but I was irritated. How could he not remember me? I booked his stupid massage sessions every week. Now I felt like a fool. Soon after, two other young guys admitted to not remembering me, but now they made a point to hang around and flirt.

This struck me as abnormal. Even if I found someone to be as attention-worthy as the color taupe, I'd at least have a vague recollection of that person's presence, if only as some kind of placeholder. Being chatted with and included as part of the team now delighted me beyond reason, but my feelings were secretly hurt. It troubled me that my accepted status had conditions and thus could be revoked. But could my own extreme shyness and sense of inferiority have made me invisible? Maybe, but here, of all places, I should've been seen as an embodied soul, not a head of hair.

My boss, Otto, was a whole different story. He was my cheerleader and expert on all matters gay, as well as my running fashion and wig consultant.

"I love it. You look fabulous! Don't let anyone tell you otherwise." Otto knew his stuff too since he'd helped his drag queen friends with their wigs for years and years. "Here's an old drag queen trick for ya: Kneel down and touch the toe of your pump, like you're fixing something, but you're really showing off how fabulous your wig is." He also offered cautionary tales. "We'd be at a drag bar, and you'd see this ball of fire behind a guy's head. You'd be kind of mesmerized at first, like oh look at the pretty orange glow, but then it kept growing, and you'd realize his hair was on fire. So, be careful around candles, honey."

* * *

Bonnie and I reunited and were back on our evening schedule, which meant searching for college guys. In order to include this young and horny demographic in our study, we decided to hang around the Columbia University area on the Upper West side.

It was just after six and hot as fuck. Our first thirty minutes were spent trying to find the B train. Sweat pooled around the base of my neck, and my black velvet dress began to drip. *You said you knew where it was! So where is it?* Inwardly, I snarled at Bonnie.

When we finally descended onto the platform, I officially entered hell. The temperature must've doubled, the train took another thirty minutes to arrive, and I had on an insulated hair hat. It kept sucking up moisture and expanding like a feral Chia pet. Since I wasn't capable of being civil, I moved to the other end of the platform.

Once we were finally on the train, I asked Bonnie to observe if my fuck-off vibe made any difference data wise. And indeed it did. Everyone gave me a wide berth, and my presence appeared to repel direct eye contact, except for one woman who kept giving me suspicious looks.

As soon as we were above ground, I bought a comb. The bodega only had a flimsy, anemic one, but it would have to

do. I walked and detangled on the way to our first stop, the Hungarian Pastry Shop, which was reported to be a popular student hangout. We did find quite a few grad student and professor types working on their laptops inside while others just lounged around on the outside patio, although I only had eyes for the bathroom. When I joined Bonnie at our outside table, a lump jumped into my throat, and tears threatened to fall. *Oh no, I can't cry!*

"I'm miserable. I look stupid; I'm hot; I'm stressed; I can't scratch my head; my emotions are all a jumble, and maybe this whole thing is a dumb idea." I tried to laugh, but it came out more like a blubber.

She gave me a hearty rallying speech and reminded me we had to do this, and I couldn't quit. That and the amazing chocolate pastry helped a little.

Then my compulsive hair grooming started up again. A handful of minutes later, I felt a tap on my shoulder and turned to look at the smiling bald man sitting behind me.

"It's been over fifteen years since someone combed my hair like that!"

I blinked at him in bafflement.

"Oh, you've been brushing your hair onto my bald head for a while now!"

"I'm so sorry! I tend to forget how long it is."

"Oh no, it's fine. It brought back fond memories, and it felt wonderful. You hair is impressive! *Very* impressive."

After the pastry shop, we continued looking for schoolboys. We entered a dark bar featuring pinball machines and groups of young beer drinkers. The two kind of cute, young bartenders bickered over who got to serve us drinks.

"He always tries to hog all the cute ones!"

This exchange lit up my world. Maybe I didn't look so hideous!

Not much young buck action was to be found, so we

moseyed downtown for about thirty blocks. I'll let the spy notes explain what happened along the way. All numbers are Bonnie's. If you want *my* side of the story, multiply them all by five.

Walking on Amsterdam:
2 teen (yarmulke-wearing) Jewish boys
1 50s dad with daughter stared up/down
4 looks from 20s girls, one disapproving
1 30s couple
8 other assorted looks from 20/30s men
1 bike deliveryman stared
1 50s gay couple
2 60s gray-haired men together stared
1 50s man eating at outdoor café
2 40s women in outdoor café
1 very tall black 40s man
2 30s guy in gym clothes stared.

We happened upon a restaurant called Fred's. We chose it as our dinner destination since it was named after someone's dog and we found that funny. It also had a great sidewalk seating area. The place was packed and oddly, most everyone seemed to be eating macaroni and cheese. From our outside perch, we watched the steady stream of passersby.

Now I felt content since the night was cooler, a touch less moist, and a slight breeze blessed our table. We ate well, drank lots of wine, made fun of me, and gathered high-quality street data.

To satisfy the night's mandatory tavern time, we had a drink at the nearby Dead Poet's Bar. Bonnie recorded her impression of the tavern in her spy notes.

This place was full of wasted regulars; all guys alone or in groups. Some clown insisted on writing me a sonnet and grabbed my stalking notebook. His friend was rolling his eyes in a, "He does this all the time" way. I know that's not data, since it was me, but it will probably make you remember the place.

When it happened, I sulked heavily as I listened to the guy babble, in mostly incoherent rhyme, about her beauty and feminine wiles. *Wait! Treason! This is supposed to be about me! I should be sitting where she's sitting!* Rationally, I knew these thoughts were defensive hooey, but a surge of angst and depression ran through me anyway. Soon, it felt as if I'd been dealt a grave blow. As he waxed badly, I wondered why he didn't choose me as his muse and write me drunken, sentimental drivel on an Amstel coaster.

I sat at the bar, sucking down vodka, and shaking with fury. My violent chain of emotional reactions shocked me. I truly wanted to kick Bonnie off her barstool. It became fairly impossible to contain my rage, so I had to calm myself down fast.

My inner shrink jumped in and asked, *What is the real problem?*

I feel irreparably defective since I'm not getting attention. I can't stand sitting here; my skin feels like it's on fire. I need a guy to talk to me.

Emergency shrink response: *Absolutely not true. These feelings go way back, has nothing to do with the drunken idiot over there; forget him. You are wonderful, valid, and loveable as is, and please don't keep up the old habit of depending on some guy to grant you the right to live.*

After getting through that maelstrom, we contemplated going into an overflowing bar full of underage and barely legal boys and girls all seriously trying to score. All of the doors and windows were open, and I was able to freely take in the horrific sight. No way could I go in there! I'd barely survived a poem drama. They'd eat me alive.

"Um... I don't know ... I mean a lot of young people are in there, so it's good for data... but ... but I think it's too horrible."

"I know. Don't worry. We can't go into that hell. We could be their mothers."

My relief sent me homeward in good spirits, and the hair hat came off as soon as I slid inside the cab and closed the door.

* * *

Date: Friday, October 7th
Fields of Research:
    Posh uptown happy hour, 5:00pm – 7:00pm
    Midtown after work bar crowd, 7:00pm – late

* * *

Fridays began at an ultra posh, high society happy hour destination. The Four Seasons Hotel bar, 5757, was the first place on my list. It was definitely up-scale and had earned a Best of New York, "Bar to Pick Up a Sugar Daddy" award.

My Friday night project outfit was a black, crocheted mini dress that had a bit of a flare to it and bell sleeves. So, dressed like I had a date with Austin Powers, I awaited my spy's arrival in the large, magnificent lobby of the hotel. Not many people passed through, but when they did, everyone discreetly looked at everyone else, in a nonchalant, casual sort of way. I had fun pretending to be a hip heiress.

Together, Bonnie and I passed through the giant lobby and main floor until we found the 5757 bar. It was very classy and built on a majestic scale, although the actual bar was itty-bitty. We chose seats at the bar itself, but most people sat at large, round tables and talked amongst themselves. This seating arrangement made me wonder how the Lycra wrapped, gold-diggers hit on their sugar daddy targets. Did they prance about from table to table? Plus, the huge room was *way* too well lit and too quiet for that kind of thing. As if to answer my question, a young woman appeared and

perched herself at the end of the little bar to shamelessly show me how to do it: drape body over everything and everyone, show off ass tattoo, drink heavily and flirt with unattractive men.

A lonely looking, middle-aged businessman sat down next to me, and we struck up a conversation. He was nice, although he depressed me with tales from his daily grind and requests for me to spice up his life. Even so, his attention, no matter how sad, perked me up.

Just as we were leaving, a handsome, thirty-something man arrived. He nodded, raised his glass, and smiled my way. I smiled wistfully in return, Bonnie yanked on my arm.

"Hey. This could lead to good research fodder!"

"You just want to flirt. Nope, we've stayed too long. We have to go and get back on schedule."

I made whining noises and objected loudly. "I want to have fun too, and he was cute."

"Get over it."

Our pressing agenda took us to a pub in Midtown called Ginger Man. It was supposed to be a boozy, beery hall filled with rowdy after-hour drinkers from the nearby offices.

Striding through the double door, I paused, poised to receive admiring looks from the throngs, but only a handful of men checked me out. Where were all of the book-worthy acts of passion? Where was the adulatory attention that was supposed to lift me out of my depression? I was getting desperate. But something didn't add up. Before the experiment started, I got way more action and adventure on my own. So it had to be Bonnie! She had to be squishing my mojo with her anti-flirting, antisocial vibe.

My spy's face had a wary, blank, and impenetrable mask aspect about it. She was the perfect visual expression of *NO TRESPASSING*. And her spy notes summarized what she was thinking under there.

This place is a hellhole of happy hour. Totally packed, games on TV above bar. Everyone in there is twenties to maybe early thirties except for a few inevitable old men ogling younger women. People are all dressed as if they came from work. It's totally the crowd that does Hampton shares and goes to Superbowl parties. (Do not read anything positive into this.)

Sure, I could see her point, and I admit to being amused, but this sucked. My sidekick's attitude didn't exactly purr *come hither*. When I hinted that she should come up with a flirting strategy, she responded, "I'll be here with you to observe, but that's it. I'm not getting paid to talk to these fools. Sorry."

As we pushed and pulled our way to the back of the bar, looking for any spare space to occupy, I kept waiting for the swooning to start. Didn't happen.

"Why the fuck am I not getting hit on?" I screamed in her ear. We were sweaty and pressed up against each other, and I wanted an answer.

"You know maybe you're having an off night or something. Happens to everybody."

That made me feel worse, but I didn't let her in on the fact that it was her fault. I needed a beverage in hand to handle this crisis. So, I squeezed in between two guys and ordered our usual vodka tonics, plus water on the side for me.

As I handed Bonnie her drink, the somewhat attractive man sitting to my right leaned in.

"I'm very impressed and a little scared that you're double fisting it. And I might have to double fist some vodka, so I won't be too intimidated to talk to you."

"Oh just drink your beer and get over it!" I giggled and beamed at him in relief. If he only knew the truth: He'd just rescued me from total *femme fatale* failure. He introduced me to his friend, who immediately asked me to pull all my hair back so he could see my face. I groaned at this new opportunity to be revealed as a fake, but I obliged. Very carefully.

"Nice. Very nice." My guy agreed and then excused himself. Upon his return, he announced, "You know, I spent the whole time in the bathroom trying to figure out if you were a real redhead."

At first I went on alert, but his loopy and smitten look reassured me he wasn't on to anything. "Well, what do you think?" I laughed.

"Well, I think it's brown, and you dyed it red. That's what I think!"

I gave him a cheeky grin and shrugged my shoulders. "Maybe." Giggle. Giggle. Giggle.

That satisfied him.

A drink or three later he asked if we wanted to go to a party with him and his friend. Bonnie had kept her distance, and he nodded her way.

"No thanks. I'm doing a social experiment, I can't."

As soon as I said this, he reared back on his barstool and shook his head violently. "You don't have a control, objective, or a plan! You go out for drinks with no preparations and call it a social experiment. YOU WILL FAIL! There's no control, there's no objective!" His eyes bugged out, and he pounded on the bar as he kept on ranting.

"Oh yes I do! If you only knew! A plan beyond your wildest dreams!" I yelled back and laughed hysterically.

During his tirade he paused a few times to pump himself up, football huddle style, by clapping his hands and shouting man sounds at the baseball game on the big-screen. He even high-fived me. "Women! And then they're all sad when they wake up in the morning and don't know who they're with. It's all their fault. It's nothing but a lack of planning!" He shook his head sadly, gave me a friendly pat on the shoulder and left.

* * *

Date: Saturday, October 8th
Fields of Research:

Union Square Afternoon street time/wandering around, 2:00pm – 5:00pm

Lower East Side late night bar scene, 10:00pm – early am

* * *

How would wearing ugly sweat pants affect data? Could my hair rise above my dumpy presentation and merit attention all by itself?

Well, our research would prove inconclusive since it rained buckets all afternoon and drenched everyone. Too many umbrellas were in the way to see anything, and the few looks I got were in the vein of "Oh, ick," but everyone else looked like a drowned rat, too.

So, after a few wet hours, we came back to my apartment, joked around and did random wig maintenance until it was time for me to get ready for a night in the rowdy Lower East Side.

I put on the black leather mini skirt, black bustier, black stockings, and black boots, then balked when I looked in the mirror.

"No way I can go out in this!" I screeched. "You know it seemed like a good idea and funny when we picked it out, but now it's too real... This skirt could reasonably pass for a belt!"

"Yep, you look like a total slut."

"Hey!"

"What? That's good. That's what you wanted."

I removed the silver linked chain that draped across my lady region and felt mildly less horrified.

It sounded like steel bullets were pelting my roof, so we

made ourselves a drink hoping that we could wait out the rain.

"I am so tired. I honestly feel like I'm dying. This can't be normal, from just going out, can it?"

"Well, you went from never going out to going out constantly, so of course you're tired."

"I know, but it's like death has sunken into my bones. You know, the kind of exhaustion that hurts."

"Why don't we skip tonight then? It's a shitty night, and we'll just make it up later."

"Oh no! I can't skip tonight! We have to stay on schedule. I can't start giving in now. And I'm sure going out in this slut-wear will put me on full, wide-awake alert." The idea of being alone and depressed scared me.

"You're probably right about that! Well, I'm good to go. I just wanted to give you an option."

Finally, we had no choice but go out in the rain. The first two men who passed by took a long look and hollered,

"Oh God Damn, look at that! Shit, Goddamn!"

"I can assure you that had nothing to do with your hair, my friend! Ha!"

"Not funny."

We arrived, once again drenched, at *Pianos Bar* around eleven. *Pianos* is a sceney bar, lounge, and live rock music venue that's very popular with the hipsters. The abysmal weather didn't keep any of them away, either. I could barely push through the front door, but once I got on the other side, I came face to face with a group of pale, young men who were all staring at me. My first instinct was to double over, cover my nakedness, and make a hasty backwards retreat, but instead I stood there, feeling tarty and exposed. That left me with no other choice but to stride up to the bar and start the heavy drinking.

As I waited for the bartender, the guys formed a semi-circle behind me and hemmed me in. I could feel their eyes not having to undress me. I was thankful when the vodka arrived. I slipped out of their noose and stood next to Bonnie a few feet away. Within five minutes, one of them came over and motioned for me to lean in so he could tell me something.

"Uh, my friend here," and he nodded his head towards the one seated at the bar, "reckons that's not your real hair."

"Well, it is!" I shot back. Instead of causing panic, his friend's reckoning really pissed me off. My get up was very costume-like, so I could see how it wouldn't take a big leap of imagination to think of my hair as an accessory, but fuck you! The messenger nodded his head in agreement and went back to the group to report his findings. I shepherded us to the other side of the room because I feared they would start tugging. And I ordered another drink.

Not good. I wanted to take the wig off and wrap it around my ass, like extra fringe, to add something to my afterthought of a skirt. Plus, Bonnie's outfit looked like nun garb compared to mine, and she acted like a woman betrothed to the almighty, too. Which was fine for her, but this wasn't normal bar behavior and didn't promote interaction. We made quite a pair.

A weathered looking old man sat hunkered down over his beer at the end of the bar. He'd been shamelessly leering for quite a while, so I started to do it back. By now I'd come to the conclusion that he was the actual old man from the sea. His big, rugged, craggy hands and ruddy, creased face told me he'd captained a ship since birth out in some far, cold ocean. Plus, he had a bushy grey beard, slate grey eyes and wore an enormous grey overcoat. Coming up with the story of how he landed here distracted me from the fact that I was here, in the same boat.

Downstairs got annoyingly packed, so we went upstairs to the lounge and dance floor. I was standing near the stairs, trying to figure out where to go, when the huge bouncer guy motioned me towards him. Instantly, I felt more attractive. Smiling coyly, I approached. Then he pointed at my ass. "Miss. Your price tag is showing. Look." And he pointed in the direction of my ass again. *Oh Jesus!* A big ole *XL $45.99* sticker was jutting straight out of my butt for all to see. Fine! I ripped off the price tag, tossed it in the garbage, and surrendered to my humiliation.

Bonnie reported a fair amount of lustful attention from men in the lounge area mixed in with horrified looks from women. On my end I can report that everything felt wrong. Damn it, Kali deserved a hot night out, and I felt cheated for both of "us."

After Pianos, we went to a candle-lit bistro and settled in a cozy back table for calamari. Lots of tables filled with very happy and drunk people spread out in front of us. This was good. The place was snug and warm, and I was pleased to be sitting down with my coat draped over my bare legs. Finally, I relaxed and we laughed about the night and the entire wacky week.

I was surprised and worried. Kali got lots of attention but no one, except for the drunken guy who accused me of not having a control, asked me out or even asked me my name. *What does a girl have to do to get a date in this town?*

Chapter III
Week Two: The Raven-Haired Woman, "Nada Jolie"

We weren't sure which wig to do next until we realized Halloween was just around the corner. That decided it. The black wig had to go public right away, or I would get lost in a sea of Morticias. My dark transformation was a shock, and it changed everything, even the weather.

Meteorologist's report from 1010 WINS News:

"The rainiest spot in the Northeast in October was the core of the Big Apple — Central Park, where 16.73 inches fell to eclipse a 102-year record of 13.31 inches. More than half that total — 8.5 inches — fell over a three-day period from Oct. 12 – 14."

* * *

Date: Monday, October 10th
Fields of Research:

 Wall Street lunch, 12:00pm – 2:00pm (Soho Substitution)
 West Village street time, 2:00pm – 5:00pm
 West Village happy hour, 5:00pm – approx 8:00pm

* * *

My skin looked sickly pale against the glossy darkness framing my face, and anything soft about me turned harsh. My eyes were sunken holes, and my entire countenance seemed to be pulled downwards by an invisible burden. I had gone from force of nature to freak of nature. I named this self, "Nada Jolie." Translation: nothing pretty.

My all-black business suit didn't quite meet Wall Street professional standards to begin with, and with the new wig, I looked Office Goth.

When I arrived at noon, Wall Street was abandoned. I wondered what calamity had struck until Bonnie greeted me with the news that it was Columbus Day. We walked around, searching for pockets of people, and only found a weirdly depressing street fair that featured mostly smoking hunks of meat. The few businessmen we did happen upon blinked their eyes rapidly and showed other signs of surprise when they spotted me.

Women pursed their lips and clucked to themselves. After passing through the rows of hanging sausages, we decided to go to Soho and come back the next day.

When we walked into a Starbucks in Soho, I spotted the Kermit guy hunkered down in the same seat as last week. He couldn't get enough of me then, but now he never looked my way. Kermit must have a thing for redheads.

Two coffees later, I had no choice but to join the inevitably long bathroom line. After putting in my twenty-minute wait, a middle-aged man, wearing a suit and barking into his cell phone, attempted to saunter right in ahead of me. Immediately, I moved forward, cleared my throat loudly, and gave him an evil look. He flinched and then fled. The older, well-dressed woman standing to my right congratulated me on putting my foot down.

"Oh, I would've eaten him alive if he went through with it, believe me," I told her. She snickered but then scooted ever so slightly away.

After Starbucks, we got back on schedule and headed towards the West Village for our street time stint. The weather had turned foul: drizzling, cold, and dismal. As we went along under the mist, people glared, and I didn't even get one even one flirty look.

"Do women really need to openly scoff at me?"

"I have to admit I'd probably smirk, too. I'd think, 'You're thirty-three, and you're still a Goth girl? Please!'"

Around the subway hub at West Fourth Street, we passed a large group of actual Goth kids, cloaked entirely in black except for the silver piercings, dog collars, and random spikes that added touches of shiny brilliance. Some of them appeared puzzled, and others pointed and quipped at my appearance. I found myself in a weird social limbo; I appeared Goth to non-Goths and non-Goth to Goths. I was an unclassified spectacle.

Gone was the attention that had fueled me, and my withdrawal was severe. As we spent the hours strolling around and drinking coffee, I felt increasingly lonely, and my foghorn of existential angst was becoming too loud to ignore.

Happy hour arrived, and we spent it installed in a booth at the old White Horse Tavern. A handful of people drank at the bar, and a few sat at tables. We ordered Irish coffee, to warm up our wet, clammy selves, and learned that Dylan Thomas partook of his last whiskey binge here. Legend has it he downed eighteen shots, stumbled out the door and died the next morning. I don't know what his problem was because he had a great head of hair, but I felt his pain regardless and decided to write a poem. When I finished, I pushed my notebook toward Bonnie.

"Here. I'm going for the genre of Teenage Goth Girl," I announced.

...Thunderheads roll and drench
the garden of thorns with the essence of pain, but leave the roses alone

to wither and curse all their lovely names.

"Good job. That's some pretty horrible high-school poetry there."

She had just congratulated me, but it hurt my feelings. I had kind of tried.

We resumed an ongoing conversation, which was, of course, about my boyfriend.

"We have *no* sex life," I told her about my boyfriend, Tim. "He's good for me; sweet, kind, and my best friend. I could never break-up with him."

Tim and I had met at a loft party in Chelsea when I was brand new to the city, over three years before. He was alone, hovering near the snack table. I was alone, standing in the middle of the room. My first impression was that he looked kind and friendly, in need of someone to chat with, and too nerdy to be a jerk. Geeky and nice was perfect for me since I was horribly insecure, didn't really know anyone, and was about to run away. Then I decided, to my relief, that he was tall and substantial enough and even kind of adorable. He was someone I could go out with. He could be my savior. When I introduced myself and noticed he had bits of white, creamy dip stuck in the corners of his smile, I knew he was the one for me.

That was three years ago, but Tim hadn't been blown away by the new me. It creeped him out that I was wearing someone else's hair. When I told him about my plans for Crowning Glory, he was *mostly* supportive and relieved I would have a project.

"Don't think I don't know that this whole thing is an excuse to flirt with men," he said.

"Come on, it's an experiment! And you know how desperately I need something to do. Sure, I admit I like the attention, but nothing else is going to happen."

We both laughed off the issue, behaved like buddies, and did that night's crossword together in bed.

After another drink with Bonnie I added, "I so want excitement and adventure, but if I leave, who will be there to take care of me if I fall into depression again?" After another twenty minutes, "Oh God, if I don't have wild sex soon I'm going to DIE!"

"This is a tough one. You're right, I'm not sure you could find someone else to be there for you like that, and being bored out of your mind sucks, but you're *not* going to *die*. After a few drinks you always go from 'I love him,' to 'I'm going to die.'" Bonnie rolled her eyes at me intensely and often. It ended up becoming a joke between us.

When I returned to the table after a bathroom trip, Bonnie leaned in urgently and whispered.

"I don't know what happened, but the whole row of guys at the bar almost fell off their stools trying to get a better look at you on your way back just now."

We decided to call it a night. As I stood up, I instinctively smoothed out the back of my skirt only to discover it was tucked snugly into my sheer tights. Then I remembered something. Getting ready took more time than I'd planned on this morning, so I hurried and went commando.

When I got home, I felt like crying. I had a hard time disassociating myself from Nada and all of the negativity sent my way. Feeling like an outcast hurled my thoughts back to my most painful period of real-life social rejection.

* * *

At the end of the year 2000, I was hospitalized after a prolonged psychotic break. There I was diagnosed as bipolar and medicated to the gills. Once released, I remained in downtown Chicago to be close to my doctors. I lived in an impersonal and suffocating one-room apartment on the top floor of a hotel, and my mother moved in to help take care of me.

As a result of side effects from the medication, I gained seventy pounds. I went from a size six to a size sixteen in two months, from one hundred and thirty-five pounds to two hundred and five. I couldn't stay in one size for more than a week, and my stylish, fitted clothes were traded for long, embroidered Indian dresses found at flea markets; the boxy, shapeless ones with tie-backs.

One morning, after I showered, my mother came out of the bathroom holding a large, dark clump in her palm.

She looked horrified as she said in an urgent and alarming voice, "Look, Stacy! You're losing your hair!"

I stared at the dripping ball in her hand and felt a sick kick in my gut. Cold panic washed over me at the reality in front of me. "NO I'm NOT! No I'm NOT! I'm not losing my hair!" I yelled at her defiantly.

"Yes, you are Stacy. Yes, you are! LOOK!" She shoved the clump towards me, insistently.

We both stared in disbelief.

Crying and screaming, I ran to the mirror and studied what I saw as I ran my fingers through the thin strands. More and more came out. I didn't even recognize myself. My face, my hair, my body were now unwelcome strangers, invaders, identity rapers. I felt wild and hopeless, miserable and furious. I wanted to die. *This can't be happening to me*, my mind pleaded over and over. And I had no immediate fix I could come up with since I had no control over the situation.

So there I was, a young woman sharing a hotel bed with her mother and leading a life that revolved around a hospital. I felt like shit, I didn't know anyone, I was gaining weight exponentially, and now I was losing my hair.

My hair kept falling out. I went to Vidal Sassoon with the hopes that something could be done with what was left. The stylist convinced me to go radical. He wanted to "give me an edge." Anything would help, I figured. He dyed my hair burgundy and shaved everything up to within a couple inches of the crown, but left the top layer long, hanging down to about mid-ear. Basically, I got a punk skateboarder cut, and it was hideous. My face looked even more bloated than before. When the wind blew, I was bald with sorry, thin red wings flapping about.

That winter in Chicago was the loneliest and worst period of my life. Eventually, I moved from the hotel to a posh, yuppie apartment building—complete with doormen—where everyone was young, wealthy, and attractive. It was the best option I had at the time, but at that place, even the doormen shunned me. The old man who ran the deli downstairs was the only person who was nice to me in the six months I lived there.

I'm sure my depression and insecurity played a part in being treated poorly, since even my ability to interact with people disappeared, but it really came down to what I looked like. Who wanted to be friends with an obese, morose-looking, mostly bald woman? I didn't. My self-worth was covered in fat and my self-confidence had fallen out.

This killed my pride. Since the dawn of my late blooming, I'd been a girl who always got noticed. I had become a purple muumuus wearer and was unwanted. Worse yet, in the past, I had always used my sexuality to get attention from men, to boost my low self-esteem, and to give myself a sense of identity, but all of that was gone. People looked at me with disdain, if they looked at me at all. No one helped me in stores, did little nice things, or chatted with me. *If they only knew why*, I kept thinking, but would that have changed anything?

This experience was long behind me. I could take the wig off, and I had my hair, body, and cheekbones back, but I still felt exposed. I had become ugly again.

* * *

Date: Tuesday, October 11th
    Fields of Research
    Wall Street Make-up Day 12 – 2 pm
    Open Center 2- 6pm
    Soho Dinner and Bar frequenting, 6:00 pm – 11:00 pm

* * *

Wall Street was back to normal, and somehow I convinced myself that men noticed me because I was hot and not just as an anomaly. This illusion lasted until I saw a forty-something woman whose long, jet-black hair matched her professional black business suit; even I couldn't help but stare and had to admit she looked odd at best.

Bonnie and I walked into a crowded restaurant and the hostess's face froze in a half-smile at the sight of me. Her expression changed to a haughty smirk.

"I'm sorry, I can only accommodate you with outside seating at this moment. We are full." Her eyes never left my forehead. I had experienced men talking to my breasts but never a woman talking to my hairline.

"It's too cold outside. No thanks." I turned on my heel and left.

Once outdoors, it didn't seem so chilly after all, and the location provided good people watching, so we took a table. A bit later, the hostess ventured out and spotted us. The next thing I knew she was bent down, right to the level of my head.

"You see, it wasn't that bad out here, now was it." Still doubled over, with her hands on her knees, she took a baby step backwards and fixed her eyes on my scalp. And stayed there far too long. I wanted to slam her face into the picnic table. I waited for her to leave. With a smug smile, she finally straighted up and left. She didn't give a damn.

"How rude! She just blatantly gathered her own wig data on me!"

"That she did," Bonnie agreed.

"This is weighing on me. I feel so badly disrespected, and it's been such a huge let down from all the attention I got last week. I miss being Kali. I'm depressed. I'm not getting noticed in a good way and …"

Bonnie seemed distracted and distant. Her face wore that impenetrable mask of hers. "I think if you take this attention and this experiment personally, then it's going to be to your own detriment," she flatly replied. "I'm saying this for your own well-being."

We parted ways for the afternoon.

It started to rain again, so I pressed myself against the wall of a nearby building and tried to think of a way to keep my spy from quitting.

The evidence overwhelmed me. The night before at White Horse, I'd asked her questions about her boyfriend and friends. She happily told me about them, and it was all perfectly normal, but I felt so devastatingly lonely, and I wanted to be her friend for real so badly that I was worried I'd come across as desperate, like I was trying to infiltrate her social circle. When I got home from the bar that night, I wanted to fix things, so I sent her a babbling text message reassuring her I wasn't trying to buy her friendship.

And now she'd just given me a fed-up admonition. After a week of this, she must be convinced the "book" would never exist. I was just an egocentric, crazy woman. She'd barely spoken today, probably because she didn't know how to break the news yet and figured it would be easier to quit later, over cocktails. If she abandoned ship, everything would sink.

I could barely breathe.

The little ledge didn't give me much shelter. I was wet and cold, but I didn't move until I'd sent her three text messages promising that the experiment was real, that I would try not to take things so personally and to please not quit.

She replied, "All is well."

God, I hoped so, but maybe she was just waiting to resign in person.

With a bit of composure gained, I stopped at a café, changed into my Tuesday casual pants outfit in the café bathroom, and arrived an hour late for my shift at the Open Center. No one cared about my tardiness.

"Is that your real hair?"

"No."

"Well, good."

"If the color weren't so black, I mean if it were softer, you could pull it off. But that looks like one of those women who have processed and processed until their hair's like shiny leath-ah," said the resident energy-healer in her thick Bronx accent.

"Take that off!" This from the friendly receptionist, "Just take that off! Girl, you're tearing me up. I just want to come in there and take it off your head! You look like a vampire!"

Upon my entrance into the wellness office, Otto silently motioned me to give him a profile view, a head-on shot and then to do a little catwalk before he passed judgment. "Oh you're hot all right, but I think you should go even paler."

"Paler? I already look dead. You're insane."

"Well, if ya got a look, you gotta work it honey. That's all I'm saying. It's working, but go paler and darken your eyebrows."

Otto distracted me for a while, but my nerves began to crack as the time to reunite with Bonnie drew near. My mind, aka super-charged chaos machine, had been smashing up my thoughts for the last few hours. Everything felt like a gigantic, big deal. I couldn't gauge how I truly acted or how Bonnie and I were getting along. I vowed to put some professional distance between myself and the experiment, and that included Bonnie, too. I would focus on the task at hand.

* * *

"Hi. I'm sorry. You're right; I can't take this personally, and I know it's just a wig. I swear I'm serious about the experiment; I'm not just a crazy attention seeker." This blurted out as soon as I saw her.

"No. I'm sorry. I didn't mean to give off any bad vibe. Really, I just felt tired and out of it and a bit glum because of the weather."

Things seemed ok between us. To keep it that way, my goal for the night was to keep my mouth mostly shut. We soldiered through our night of Soho barhopping and got a dozen weird looks, two scant traces of interest, and a pair of wet clothes to show for it.

* * *

Date: Wednesday, October 12th
    Fields of Research:
    Midtown power business lunch, noon – 1:00pm
    Midtown to Upper West Side street time, 1:00pm – 2:30pm
    Upper West Side loitering, 2:30pm – 4:00pm

* * *

"It's Power Lunch Wednesday," I reminded myself as I lay in bed and refused to budge. Was I such a wuss that going out felt life-threatening? *GET UP!*

All right, Nada, we need to come to some kind of an agreement.

I reappraised myself after I finished darkening my eyebrows and popped in some light grey contacts. Nice. Smoky eyes and smoky brows went so much better with sooty hair.

Changing eye color wasn't part of my original experimental plan, but I decided if it helped me feel less ridiculous, and thus less paranoid, any loss in scientific integrity would be justified. And, since it was so cold, I added a frilly black sweater to my artistic dress outfit. It made me think of gypsies, spies, and dramatic Italian women. Nada and I were going to get along, damn it.

My umbrella cried uncle as soon as I walked out the door. This sideways, wind-driven, torrent had really gotten out of hand. I felt pity for myself. Poor Nada had been rained on the entire time. But onwards I went to our fittingly named business lunch hotspot, Oceana.

A pale-skinned, paunchy priest stood next to me on the subway. After glancing at me a few times, he resolutely gripped the bar and stared ahead with a troubled look. Our gazes met as I exited. He gave me a slow shake of the head and lowered his eyes. This put a smile on my face and a spring back into my step.

Once above ground, two delivery boys walked behind me talking about my appearance in Spanish. I couldn't hear everything, but I caught certain key words and phrases.

"...Body", "...wet", "...pretty hair", "can't see her ass very well though."

By the time I arrived at Oceana, I looked like I'd crawled out of one. I found Bonnie seated at a table soaking in her own puddle.

"Hi. I'm not happy. I've never felt so disgusting. And have you noticed that this place is decorated and even shaped like a ship, complete with painted portholes? It's so stuffy, and those are the only 'windows' in here. We can't escape this water theme." Her expression showed no trace of amusement.

"Um, now that you mention it, I do see we are in a boat."

The handful of other diners, mostly women in power suits, appeared crisp, highly put together and boring. They ignored us for the most part. The staff, on the other hand, would not leave us alone.

"Someone always seems to be right behind me. There are at least seven people serving us. It's unbearable." Bonnie was surly.

Our seafood lunch arrived, and I thought everything tasted bland and wet but didn't want to say anything.

"Didn't you read they had, like, the best seafood in the city? I hate to say this, but this food sucks." Bonnie picked at her fish with a frown.

"I'm sorry, but it's not my fault. Blame Zagat's."

Then we both fell silent, and I began thinking of the dead, drowned girl from *The Ring*, crawling out of the well.

On our way out, I couldn't find my coat check ticket, and that upset the host. I chatted and giggled with the coat check girl and finally dumped everything out of my purse—including lint, spare change, and a tampon—right onto her counter. The host's attempts to help me became serious, and his smile turned even less believable. By the time I finally got my coat, he was gritting his teeth and glaring at the girl, so I smiled at him and kept on carrying on with her.

"He so wanted me out of there! That was actually kind of fun!" I yelled at Bonnie as we ran back into the rain.

We installed ourselves in a crowded Barnes & Noble café uptown since monsoon street time was not an option.

A redheaded boy, maybe three or four years old, put his crayon down, swiveled around in his chair, and gawked at me.

"Mommy, what's that?" he asked in his outside voice.

"Well, honey, maybe she's an Aborigine," his redheaded mommy looked at me and answered without skipping a beat. Her child bounced up and down in his seat and kept pointing.

"Or maybe she's Native American. That's it, sweetie. She's Native American. You know what that is, right honey?"

He nodded his head and then merrily went back to coloring.

Mommy and I locked eyes. She didn't even flinch or smile.

Bonnie and I decided that the boy was too young to understand the term "freak" and that he'd probably just had a Native Peoples of the World theme week at pre-school. I worked hard to convince myself that she didn't know it was a wig and perhaps had astutely observed that I am one sixty-fourth Cherokee. Did I look so strange that small children failed to recognize me as human?

The mall that had been packed with psychics last week was empty today, probably due to armageddon weather, so we visited a wig parlor next door. The walls of the entry area were lined with autographed photos of stars, and only a few wigs on display behind glass cases. We thought this was a store, but it looked more like an upscale hair salon. I didn't think we should go in, but it was too late.

"May I help you?" the young woman behind the front desk called out. Her tone and inflection indicated we must be lost.

"Hi. Do you have any flesh-colored, opaque wig caps?" She shook her head no and pulled out two different styles to show me.

"All we have is this regular tan, sheer cap or this opaque, white one."

"I need something flesh-colored because you can see my real, dark hair through the back of my blonde wig, but I guess I'll take a white one just in case I can't find anything else." She had not mentioned the wig I had on my head, so neither did I.

"That'll be three dollars." Regarding me in a very peculiar manner, she handed over the cap.

We asked her what kinds of wigs were sold here. She explained that 'lace-fronts' actually have lace hairlines that are trimmed to fit and then glued on. "That's what Beyoncé and Tyra Banks wear. They're the most expensive but the most realistic. We specialize in personal fittings and only work with lace-fronts."

Oh dear, mine was a lace-less, one-size-fit-most, eBay Buy-It-Now special.

She glanced at the two older women being tended to in the salon and stiffened noticeably. "You have to make an appointment here."

I thanked her for the cap and then scurried us out of there.

"I'm sure she didn't want those ladies to think they did this to you!" Bonnie said.

"Hey! Stop it. I don't look that bad! Maybe she didn't even know."

Bonnie found that notion very funny.

But somewhere, despite the scoffing and doom, I harbored a dark glee. A more exotic and mysterious woman began to emerge. Being a freak could be fun, too.

* * *

Date: Thursday, October 13th
Fields of Research:
    East Village lunch, noon – 2:00pm
    Open Center 2 – 6 pm

* * *

A handsome gentleman with a dignified ponytail of gorgeous, silver hair sat next to me. He was tall, robust, and wore khaki National Geographic-photographer gear. He had been staring at me since he walked into the Astor Place Starbucks.

As soon as he set his wet umbrella down, I moved my leg forward so his hand could accidentally brush against my knee. *Damn, just missed.* I felt his eyes resting on my face and neck. Tingles spread through my body. He moved in close and lingered; I almost fainted from the turn-on. We locked eyes. Then, he walked out the door and disappeared into the driving rain without me. My fantasy fizzled and sent me back to the reality of my love life.

A girl with orange, spiky hair and trippy clothes came in and interrupted my thoughts. She had me beat in the weird department, but it is New York City, and the East Village at that, after all. She was overtly trying to look bizarre, whereas I may have appeared to be an unfortunate accident.

This was the first day I started to have a little fun with my dark appearance, and already I had picked up a little lascivious attention. As I pondered this, a blue-haired young man, studied me from the corner. He motioned in my direction to the orange-haired girl and her pink-haired friend. Now they were all staring.

I scooted over and joined Bonnie for a little break from the scrutiny. Something was bothering me that I wanted to get off my chest.

"On my way here, I was forced to listen to some guy on the cab radio ranting about how we've become a "check society." No one knows how to do anything, and no one helps one another anymore. We only send money; we only write a check. Now I feel really guilty. This project is so silly and trivial."

"We're not saving any babies with this, Stacy, that's for sure."

Ouch. That hurt. I wanted to have something to offer. "Yes, but without some silliness and humor in the world things would be pretty bleak, no? And maybe this will become a successful book, *and* this will open the door to my 'deeper' art."

Bonnie laughed. "Yeah, and then you can write a check."

Ok. Henceforth my spy shall be called 'Agent Thorn' in recognition of her being a thorn in my side. She further thwarted me by being quite pleased with her new code name.

* * *

My days of being invisible at the Open Center were definitely over. I was a source of entertainment, a one-woman, circus sideshow. People stopped to chat, offer up opinions, and hear the latest. The young, hippie chic who worked the volunteer shift before me, made a painful, howling noise when I entered our office.

"What is up with you and these wigs? She recoiled as if I'd just punched her.

"Well, I'm doing an experiment about hair color..." I tried my best to sound convincing and sane, but she wasn't buying it.

"Well, I hated the red wig. Oh God, it was awful! The color was a blue red or an orange red, I'm not sure which, but I just can't stand that color. I like the black one better. It suits you." She scrunched her face up as if she were looking at something gross.

"What are you talking about?" Otto yelled from across the room. "We like the red one. You're crazy; she looked sexy! Of course, this one has its charms, too. It's definitely got an S&M vibe. One look at you and you know you have a dungeon at home. You look like a woman who wants a stalker!"

* * *

Date: Friday, October 14th
Fields of Research:
    Visit to Mama Marie, psychic 12 – 2 pm
    Posh uptown happy hour 5:00pm – 7:00pm
    Midtown after work bar crowd, 7:00pm – late

* * *

After my free psychic reading at the mall last week, I thought it would be funny to get a different extra-sensory report each week. Would my appearance influence how my fortunes were predicted? The idea didn't really make comparative sense since each week I would have to visit a new psychic, but it would work fine for pseudo science.

Otto knew about these things and gave me the names of a few places in the West Village. So, on Friday afternoon I trekked alone in the rain, in search of Zena the Clairvoyant. Otto's directions were terrible, and when I finally arrived at Zena's door I was freezing, wet, and beside myself. The fancy, gilt sign said "Open" but the door was locked, and no one answered my thirty bell rings. Bitter but determined, I set out for a nameless place that was located, "...you know, next to that voodoo store."

Eventually, I found the voodoo store and a pink, neon sign that read, "Cup of Tea." I did a casual walk-by and saw the storefront window was full of crystal balls and mystical tchotchkes. A fat, old woman sat inside at a small table with a deck of Tarot cards spread out in front of her. Standing under an awning nearby, I told myself I'd come too far to chicken out now. I feared I must look extra weird because a table of eight had just pressed their faces against a café window to look at me.

A gigantic and intimidating Germanic looking man stood under the awning with me and was talking on his cell.

"Ok, talk soon and much, much love, my dear."

I figured he had to be nice to say that, so I approached him. "Can I ask you a favor?"

"Sure." He gave me a friendly smile.

"Is my wig on right? Is it lopsided, or does the hairline need to go up or down?" I blurted this out as if it were a normal question.

"Um, let me see." He laughed and stepped back to get a better look, studied my head intently, and then returned to tug it down and scooted it over to the left for me. "There. Perfect." We both cracked up.

"Thanks!" Now I could go face my fate.

* * *

The old woman waved me in and motioned for me to sit at her little table.

"Hello, honey, I'm Marie, and that is my granddaughter," she nodded to the young, dark-haired woman who was doing a reading for a young man. "Both of my granddaughters read, but I've been here for over twenty years. Back in Romania, all the women in my family are seers. We'll wait until she's done, but don't worry, I'm going to take care of you, sweetie." She took my hand in hers and held my gaze in a vice grip. Her eyes were sharp and beady, like those of a bird of prey. Marie's face wasn't one of a kindly babushka; her wrinkles were crafty. "I'm an old, tough broad, I've seen everything, more than you can imagine."

Her hand waved dismissively at the air and everything I couldn't understand. She lit a cigarette with her free hand and took a deep drag. As I watched her, I could hear her mind clicking, measuring me, sizing me up through the clouds of smoke.

"What does 'Cup of Tea' mean?" I took my hand back.

"Oh, we read your future from the grinds left on the bottom of your tea cup. It's an ancient practice. But that's not what you need today, honey. You need a full reading: palm, face, and tarot. Anything else would leave me with an incomplete picture, and I truly want to help you today." She re-clasped both her hands around mine.

My instinct was to recoil, but I was caught in her magnetic stare. And I was paranoid about my wig.

Maybe, if I didn't move, she wouldn't notice.

"My readings are different. I use my psychic gifts and intuition along with the cards to see into the heart of your real story. The cards I use aren't the classic tarot but animal totems. I read each one for their individual meaning, as well as in relation with the others and then as a whole."

Part of me wanted to get up and go, but I agreed to stay.

I cut the cards and she re-shuffled them in a few quick flutters. Then, she laid them out, one by one, until all the animals were staring at us. She mumbled to herself and poked at them with her weathered fingers. "Yes, yes, the wolf and the raven, followed by the horse. Ok sweetie, I see you have real talent, yes, and you're not here by accident; you're here on this planet to make a difference… but I see a darkness from your past, so much sadness… Oh and I see you have many, many ideas and irons in the fire, but you have to complete them or you will be burned." She looked up and winked at me, "I'm right, aren't I honey?"

"Yes, yes, that's right."

She winked at me again. Her answer to everything I said was the same; *I know, I know, honey.*

Marie pushed two cards away from the others with a sad shake of her head. "Oh sweetie, look, here it is; this is what's holding you back. A dark force, a troubled, even evil spirit, came into your life six years ago. Am I right?"

Without meaning to, I nodded my head incredulously.

* * *

Six years before, at the end of 1999, was when my life first lost its grasp on reality. Like the man in *A Beautiful Mind*, I couldn't distinguish fact from fantasy because all my senses told me what seemed impossible was real, even when the dwindling rational part of me begged to differ. How could I help getting scrambled when I saw, smelled, felt, tasted, and heard things that aren't supposed to exist?

Six years later, I still wasn't convinced that everything that had happened to me fell into the category of psychotic break or could be explained away by it. I wanted the supernatural to have been involved. I wanted to believe I had tapped into an invisible world, and that I had come out of my year down the rabbit hole with secret knowledge, inexplicable maybe, but invaluable. It would be unfair and heartbreaking if I had only lost my mind.

* * *

"You have the power to achieve anything you want, but I see this disturbing darkness around you also. This worries me, honey." Marie stubbed out the cigarette and fixed me with her hawk eyes. "Would you let me help you finally put this darkness behind you? I don't want it to beat you, honey. Let me at least do an investigation and see what can be done. It's usually fifteen hundred dollars, but I'll do it for you for five hundred."

"What? I can't pay that! Sorry." This snapped me out of it.

"Sweetie, sweetie, you've carried this darkness for six years. You know it's true. I can help you."

"No, I just can't."

"I have to buy special candles and go to my church to

pray all night, for three straight nights while they burn, so I can connect with my higher-ups and much, much more, to find out exactly where this force came from and how to clear this energy for you. Sweetie, have you ever seen a special candle?" She got up and swung open a floor to ceiling sized cabinet. "Now this is just one. I have to buy six of these for you." The candle was white, covered with thick wax vines and tall as a tree. "You have my word which is my gold, and you have my hand, which is my honor. Just give me what you can now, and I will do this. Then you come back, and I'll tell you what I found out. And you'll see, we'll put this behind you. And then you'll want to make Mama Marie a nice gift." She took me for a hundred and eighty dollars.

After I left, I kicked myself for being such an idiot and decided to scrap the whole psychic readings idea. I was way too easily taken in this area. And there would be no mention of this to Agent Thorn.

"Can I ask you a couple of questions?" a loud voice startled me out of scolding myself. I looked up to see two men, one with a camera and microphone, a few feet in front of me. Both were pressed under a ledge, hiding from the relentless rain. One smiled and stepped out of the doorway.

"Hi. Can I ask you a couple of questions? And oh wow, I just have to stop you, because you have such a great look! Really amazing. So, I'm asking people questions about addiction. It's for a documentary."

I eyed him and wondered what bullshit he was up to, but flattery will get you everywhere, and I figured it'd be good for research.

"Can I fix my hair before you ask me though?"

"Absolutely. You have such thick hair you know. Amazing."

"I know! It's such a bear to work with!" I laughed as I tried to unglue the soaked, black strands from my face.

"Would you like to go someplace dry? Or we could just do it here on the sidewalk."

I shrugged my shoulders. "I'm already wet."

"Ok, great, now get rid of that umbrella."

I didn't count on that detail, but I stood there under the rain, waiting for the cameraman to get with it, and wondered if my look was so great because it screamed drug addict.

"Ok, now just relax and here we go. Do you think America has a drug addiction problem? Do you think it is a disease?"

I decided to put effort into it. The rain stung my eyes while I put my thoughts together.

"I think it's a spiritual crisis; an existential angst that we don't know what to do with, so we fill the hole with so many things, and drugs are just one of them." I continued pondering aloud until I completely confused myself and stopped talking.

"So, what would you tell people who feel this emptiness? What could they do to fill this void?"

I looked at him and shrugged. "I don't know!"

He beamed at me anyway, and when we finished he seemed thrilled.

"You're wonderful, thank you, absolutely wonderful and great look, great look! It'll be a documentary on the Discovery channel or TLC."

It then occurred to me that my potential television debut would be as Nada, standing in the rain. I pictured my parents watching the program a year or two from now and trying to figure out why this weird woman looked so familiar:

Marsha, come take a look at this idiot they're talking to now...
Oh dear, Milton, I think that's Stacy.

* * *

Over cocktails at the Waldorf Astoria that evening, I recounted a tightly edited version of my visit with Mama Marie to Agent Thorn. Even though I left out incriminating details, Thorn still regarded me with an arched eyebrow.

"What? It was just a normal reading."

"So, it was like twenty or thirty dollars?"

I nodded in agreement, but I felt my face give me away. My eyes flew wide open and my forehead tightened, lifting the corners of my eyebrows up along with it. "It doesn't matter. I'm not going to do this again, anyway. I'm an easy target. And she freaked me out. I still feel unsettled."

"Why? She sounds like she was almost comically bad."

"Oh, she told me about how some evil spirit entered my life six years ago. Very weird things did start to happen at that time. Not too long after that, I lost my mind. I really don't know what I believe, but I have way too much questionable material in my past to play around with this stuff."

"Yeah, you're right. It's probably not a good idea, but I wouldn't worry about what she said. Everyone gets told they have some dark spirit from the past that's still clinging onto them."

I had to look away so she wouldn't see *I fell for it* written across my face. "It's not really what she said that got me I guess, it was more the whole subject of other worlds and realities that stirred up bad memories and unresolved, unsteady feelings. I'm afraid of myself. It's like living in a house with foundations that keep crumbling. I don't trust my mind, so I can't count on myself to provide a balanced and safe home base for long. That's why it's so important for me to do and finish this project now, while I can."

"You're doing really great, though. We haven't missed a day."

"I used to have eight months to a year 'off' between cycles, but last time I only got four months. And I've read that it can get worse as you get older. I never should've Googled 'bipolar.'

"My hope is that doing this project, having a schedule and a goal to work towards will give me enough of a toehold to keep from getting sucked back in. I can't really think about it though, or I'll panic."

"I think having a steady schedule, every day like this will help a lot. And we'll get through the experiment. I'm here to help."

"Thank you. I never thought I'd get this far, and here we are."

We toasted to that, but as I sipped, I wasn't sure she understood.

"Seriously," I said. "And I'm sure this won't happen, but if I start acting weird, say I'm talking about aliens or mention being the Queen of Egypt, well, you might need to call someone. Let me give you my parents' phone numbers. And I'll give you Tim's. Well, I might as well give you my doctor's number, too." I wrote 'Egyptian/Alien Hotline' on the top of the paper and handed it to Agent Thorn. "They'll know what to do. And try to keep me corralled in the meantime."

"Ok. No problem." Thorn tucked it into her spy notebook.

I felt much better. The lights were low here in the beautiful, mahogany-paneled bar. My black, crocheted mini-dress belonged in Austin Power's pad, not here, and I was still damp from the rain. I sipped my drink and tried to eavesdrop on men in expensive suits. It irked me that no man made any moves. This behavior didn't live up to my expectations of high drama. Thirty mintues went by slowly. I was bored. The proper, ancient bartenders implementing old-fashioned, shiny brass bar paraphernalia were the only entertaining things going on.

As much as I worried and complained, a spark had been ignited within me. I was living. And I was having fun! A little pilot light of happiness twinkled inside.

1 unpleasant look from young woman on way through lobby
When we entered bar:
2 from old men

2 from disapproving men
1 old guy looked from across the bar
1 fat business guy
1 horrified look from old woman
1 20's model-looking girl next to us looked
4 disapproving looks as we left dining room
3 more looks leaving hotel

* * *

The rain still hadn't given up falling. After leaving the Wal-dorf, we spent most of the next hour in the deluge trying get a cab. The city streets seemed darker, yet shone with the glow from hundreds of headlights beaming off the wet pavement. The high-rises of Midtown contributed to the gritty, *film noir* feel.

We headed back to the Ginger Man, and after just a step or two inside, Agent Thorn judged the place as one of the official circles of hell. Good God, that attitude sitting next to me would scare every man away. We made a ridiculous pair. I searched; she shunned. I beckoned; she blocked. Apparently, she was much saner than I and didn't need attention from male strangers to make her feel good. But, I did, damn it. I wanted it not only for neurotic reasons but also for research reasons and maybe even for organic, sexual ones, too.

"We have to be friendly and flirt a bit. It's for the sake of the research!"

"But I thought you wanted to count the looks you get, and who approaches *you*."

Sadly, there seemed no way to get her to play the game with me.

* * *

Date: Saturday, October 15th
Fields of Research:
Union Square Afternoon street time/wandering around, 2:00pm – 5:00pm
Lower East Side late night bar scene, 10:00pm – early am

* * *

The clock read 8:30 am. What was I doing awake at this hour? This was unusual, and something felt different. As I lathered up in the shower, I looked out the window and saw blue sky. Sunlight had awoken me! My God, I would be dry today! I pulled on my low-key, puffy Saturday sweats.

Union Square brimmed with happy people, and the day was fantastically beautiful. Despite feeling like the big girl in the back row of a Richard Simmons's *Sweatin' to the Oldies* video, I was in a good mood. Rain or shine didn't make a big difference stat-wise. I still failed to catch many eyes. I didn't care, but I did have a problem.

Bonnie was off-duty tonight due to previous plans. No one I called was available, and barhopping alone in that outfit was out of the question. I did have plans for a drink with my friend, Nikoleta, early in the evening, but she was gorgeous and intimidating. I could not imagine telling her about the experiment much less asking her to help out.

After enough street time had been logged, I joined my boyfriend, Tim, for a late lunch. We sat in a booth and smiled at each other stupidly. What to say? I hadn't seen him for a week. My days and nights were all about going out without him, and for his part, he had consistently turned down my half-hearted offers to get together. Now I felt guilty about complaining so often to Bonnie that he bored me.

The waitress came and broke our silence. She sweetly took his order and then switched to bitchy when she addressed me. She gave me a mean look and then she left.

"Wow. She wasn't very nice to you."

"Never mind. I'm used to it."

"So, how's your wig thing going?"

"It's good, although I have a huge problem because I don't have anyone to go out with tonight. I've called everyone I can think of. Would you please, please come out with me for just a little bit?"

Tim put his fork down, and his expression told me I was nuts. "Why do you think I want to observe guys hitting on you? And if you think I'm getting into a bar brawl for you, well, you're mistaken." He smiled ruefully and studied his chili Mac.

"Please. I know it's a ridiculous request but this is important to me. It's serious; it's for the project."

"The only way I'm going is if I get to dress up as a blind man. That way guys can stare with impunity."

"Come on, you can't be serious. We'd be a complete spectacle. And you don't know how to be blind! How are you going to drink?"

"Hey, you're not the only one who gets to have fun. Give me some credit. I'll get a cane. And I have to be the *absolute* last option. Otherwise, NO."

"Ok, ok. I know it's absurd of me to ask. But where on earth would you get a cane anyway?" We both laughed despite ourselves.

"I have my ways. And speaking of drinking, I think you're drinking too much."

"Come on. Two or three drinks a night! I'm fine."

* * *

Nikoleta was in town from Europe. This was the first time I would be going out with her alone in the three plus years we'd known each other. She was beautiful: lovely red hair, big blue eyes, gracefully lithe, and always stylish. Her inner wow-power was dazzling, too: multi-cultural, multi-lingual, multi-talented artist, actress, and singer. Next to her, I felt like a panicked whale out of water, although I reminded myself that if I could pull off a crazy experiment, I could manage to chat with a pretty girl.

* * *

Thinking about being with Nikoleta triggered memories of feeling ugly and unwanted that I couldn't ignore. During my terrible time in Chicago, living alone became almost unbearable. I'd lived abroad for many years, was used to having several roommates, and loved a community atmosphere. At one point, I decided to find roommates and move out of my depressing apartment building. I visited a couple of places and went through interviews. For one of them, I met three girls at a bar for happy hour so they could all get to know me and decide if they wanted me as a roommate. They were all pretty. One was tall and thin, with straight black hair and dressed in chic business clothes. The second girl had long blonde hair and was Barbie doll gorgeous. And the last woman was cute, weighed at least a hundred pounds less than I, and looked like a pixie. I felt like a monstrous blob.

When we all introduced ourselves, I noticed them glancing at each other uneasily. They acted polite and smiled, but it was awkward for everyone. After that uncomfortable hello, we all walked up to the bar and two guys made way for the three of them but then closed me out and left me standing in the middle of the bar. I wanted to leave. *Fuck.* I was wearing a purple velvet smock-like thing and had no business being in a happy hour meat market. Later, we sat at a table and chatted. We all knew it wasn't going to work.

No one called me back.

* * *

I put my little leather skirt on and then took it right off. This was not acceptable for Soho or Nikoleta. So I stuffed it in my purse and headed out in jeans.

Our three-kiss greeting went off without any wig disaster, and now we sipped our red wine and chatted politely. To my dismay, my facial gestures immediately began to go awry. The muscles around my mouth turned rubbery and sent my smile into spasms.

Worse, my neutral listening face threatened to twitch, so I nodded my head too much in compensation. The more time that passed, the more pressure I felt to offer an explanation for my hair. My escapades would give me something to talk about, and I was in dire need of something to say.

A wine refill went by before I chirped, "So, how do you like my wig?"

"What? What wig?" She looked genuinely shocked and grabbed onto a lock of it. "No! *Really?*"

"Yep! But don't yank on it too hard!"

"Oh my God. I had no idea! I thought your hair had just grown out and that you just looked great. Fantastic! It really is lovely."

My experiment turned out to be a big hit with her as well. We warmed up to each other, and everything was going great until she complimented me again.

"You really look wonderful now that you've lost all that weight! The past couple of years you've looked... puffy." She looked so proud to put her finger on that perfect word. "Good on you for losing it! You look very beautiful." She gave my arm an affectionate squeeze. I could tell she hadn't meant to pull the barstool out from under me, but my hurt feelings weren't so fast to recover.

Her last visits had sadly coincided with the two times I'd temporarily gone on medication that caused some weight gain. It was nothing like what happened to me in Chicago, although it was a heavy blow to my confidence. And of course, the weight had come off when she wasn't here to witness it.

She knew about my previous troubles and wanted to tell me about an "amazing" book she'd read on the subject.

"It's really controllable with a healthy diet. You should eat organic carrots and greens instead of taking those awful pills. You know, I knew it wasn't natural, that puffiness around your face. That wasn't just from food alone. It's really a shame. I'll send you this book."

Her well-meaning advice was hard to take charitably, and it was difficult not to cry. Especially since this was the first time I'd felt like her friend instead of an acquaintance.

Just moments ago, it had seemed miraculous and wonderful to go from being so shy all these years to giggling with her like girlfriends, but was it all because I was pretty enough now? What if I gained weight again? Will I have the confidence to hang-out with her? Will she even invite me out with her?

I kept up my end of our lively, fun conversation, but I was reminded again of that awful time back in Chicago. After being away for two months, I had returned twenty-five pounds lighter. My hair had grown back a bit, and I'd started to feel human again. Before I left, the doormen hadn't even looked at me, but when I showed back up to move out, they greeted me as a new tenant and were oh-so-jolly and flirtatious. I could have held it against them, but why? It felt so good to be welcome.

And now too, it felt so good to be welcome. *It's happening now! Enjoy it. Don't ruin this chance!* I might never have another one. The razor lodged in my throat loosened, and my drink helped wash it down. Crowds of preppy guys began closing in around *us*, which comforted me.

Then Nikoleta's friend, Steve, bounded up to the bar.

Steve was a blond, bright-eyed guy, partial to wearing t-shirts, jeans, and flip-flops for every occasion and could permanently pass for a frat boy. He started flirting with me right away, and I loved it.

Soon, my squished ego was pumped back up, and my mood shot skyward.

I laughed at something he said and gave my hair a flirty toss, which knocked over his pint of beer in one flick and sent it pouring into my purse. We removed the contents of my bag, skirt included, and placed them on the bar to dry. I had to explain. Nikoleta's entire face brightened, and she clapped in enthusiastic approval as I detailed my mission for the night.

"Oh God Stacy, go march yourself into that bathroom and come back in that smutty skirt of yours! You have to show us!"

"Yeah dude, you have to go put it on! I mean you can't dangle something like that in front of our faces. That's just cruel."

On my way back to the bar, I looked down and watched how the skirt barely grazed the tops of my thighs. My black boots, reaching up to my black knees, seemed way too hard-core. Lord, I felt like a swaggering, cowgirl whore.

"Stacy, why did you wait until now to put that on?" Nikoleta laughed and took pictures.

"Yes! Now that's what I'm talking about! *Off the hook!*" Steve howled. His flirting went into overdrive, although he was very disappointed when he learned my hair wasn't mine.

"Well, would it piss you off if you took a girl home and then found out she was wearing a wig?" I asked.

"I wouldn't be mad at all. It'd be a turn on. Man, are you kidding, I'm all about deception. I think it's hot."

My eyes sparkled in delight when I heard this. "Say, would you like to be my assistant for the rest of the night?"

"Hell ya! I have no idea what that means, but I'm your man. Sign me up!"

* * *

My substitute spy and I stumbled out of a cab and into the Lower East Side, drunk and behind schedule. We were on Ludlow Street, the epicenter of hipsterville. Inebriated, happy people were everywhere: on the sidewalks, in the road, and spilling out of all the bars. The moon shone, and the night felt electric. The mix of not getting rained on, booze, and Steve telling me I was 'white hot' had me all riled up. Even though he wasn't my type, Steve was the closest thing I'd had to a flirty date in years. Any hope for research objectivity flew out the window.

"Ok, I've got a plan." Steve announced as we got our bearings. "I'm going to give off a gay-friend vibe and let me try walking a couple of paces behind you... Oh score! Did you see that? You got a dozen looks right there! Man, you're so off the hook!" He walked backwards, straight ahead and sideways in a kind of twisting, bouncy lope trying to take it all in. "Wow, it's totally unreal. Guys really don't give a flying fuck that I'm with you, now do they? Those cheeky bastards, no respect at all, but of course I'm just your gay friend, mind you, or maybe they think I'm your little brother."

It was so much fun having a cheerleader, and with a guy by my side, I didn't feel as much like a hussy trolling for tricks the way I did with Bonnie.

We picked a basement bar called The Darkroom because we thought the name was appropriate, and it seemed nice and seedy. The first thing I saw as I stepped inside was a very dapper, young man leaning on a railing and staring at me. He had a coiffure of shoulder-length, brown ringlets and actually wore a pinstriped suit. He was a petite fellow, yet had a large presence. I decided he must be French. His eye-lock didn't waver, but I walked past him and into the crowd, heading for air pockets at the back of the bar.

We found a little nook of space and were busy laughing

and drinking when the French guy suddenly appeared. He sidled up next to Steve and started clapping and laughing along with him.

"Who won?" He asked us as he clapped.

Steve looked up, completely taken aback, but went along with it. "Well, she did, of course. What other outcome could there be, my friend?"

"Why?" asked the little man.

"Well, she's the funniest, the prettiest, really, and honestly, just the best."

This peculiar little guy then grabbed onto a lock of my hair and pulled it away from my face. "Yes, she has a good spirit," he declared.

My God, was I a horse up for auction? Since I didn't know how to respond, I stood there mute. And to be honest, it made me feel ridiculously special. He let go and smiled at Steve. "Well, good luck my friend."

I couldn't believe I was having a night out like this. Having drinks with Nikoleta and then cavorting with my new guy pal was a big accomplishment. I'd just done something I hadn't been able to do for over six years.

* * *

Years ago, in the midst of my first psychotic break, my sister, Hilary, took me to the mall. I'm sure she was afraid of me, but she wanted to help. I was frightened of myself as well, but I thought I could handle the outing.

As soon as we walked into the big department store we had loved back in our mall-hair days, I felt like a new dimension opened before me. Everything glistened with hints of magic. My mind raced, and I could feel the super-charged, I-Am-God juice start to pump in and drench my thoughts. Around the next corner, I was about to find heaven. *No, we're hallucinating, hold it together, this can't be true.*

I looked down at the floor and shut my eyes, but they kept getting drawn open. I couldn't keep from seeing mad beauty everywhere. Prisms of sparkles, the brightest, most exhilarating light bursts in existence, lit up the aisles. *Don't. It's not real. Not in front of Hilary... please.*

When I raised my eyes, I looked at the crystal figurines in a nearby glass display. Jeweled light filled my vision as millions of diamonds danced into my eyes. Physically, it was unbearable to witness this beauty, and at that moment, something exquisite shattered inside me. I was staring at bliss. Against my will, the most innocent and tender part of me ran out to touch it. *It's not real. Please, don't believe it. Come back! Hilary will hate me.* In another second, as my reason failed, I realized I was being sucked into insanity, again. *It's not fair. How could I not fall for this trick? It's so beautiful.*

After that, I can only recall what happened in a few, patchy dream sequences.

Sometimes, the clearest memories I have of those states are physical sensations. So, it felt like I was in the middle of the store, crouching down and covering my head in an effort to block everything out. I remember the cold touch of the floor against my hands and knees. My eyes and fingers searched the surface for the way in to that other, magical world, but I couldn't find it. The black and white tiles were too close to my face, too big and everything was too bright. The alarmed and harsh tone of my sister's voice kept getting closer and closer to my ear. Her embarrassment made a painful impression on me.

A sinking sensation in my stomach seemed to say, *You've been had.*

I have a fleeting memory of rushing out a door, but I can't recall any words until I woke up in the car. Hilary was driving and pleading with me to stop being crazy. That I do remember. And I think she was crying.

I didn't know how to articulate what I was going through. My mind was so slippery. It refused to stay on solid ground long enough for me to figure anything out let alone make things work right. And then I had this terror; like a gun pointed at my lucidity at all times. I'd fight and fight not to lose the footing of my mind, but when I did, I'd fight from my tiny pinpoint of light inside the insanity and try to break free—but to where? When I'd finally emerge, even for just a minute, it wasn't freedom that greeted me but the threat and horror of the next spiraling pull. And my solitary war would be waged again. Hundreds of times a day, I faced this siege during this first and worst, yearlong psychotic break.

I didn't have a voice. It's not that I didn't try to explain, but even when I could communicate clearly, what I was saying didn't translate. I had nothing visual I could point to, nothing to reference outside of myself to help people around me understand.

The next day, after the disastrous mall outing with my sister, Dad called me into the kitchen and told me to sit down at the table. Mom was already seated beside him.

"You know I have TWO daughters. And I am not about to let you ruin your sister's wedding! DO YOU HEAR ME? So, I want to know right now, can you handle going to Florida? Because if you can't, if you think you will do anything to upset her at her wedding, then you absolutely are not going. Do you hear me? I cannot allow this!" He pounded the table with his fist, and his face flushed with anger. He glared at me as if I were vermin to be exterminated. Mom appeared miserable, but she didn't say anything. "I'm serious, Stacy. You will NOT ruin Hilary's wedding. Can you handle going?" His voice was a hoarse, harsh bark.

Fuck you, was my first thought. Like I'm doing this on purpose. And you know, FYI, I'd rather not upset myself, too.

It was such a ridiculous request, that I found it pathetically funny, but I hated him and his ugly, rage-colored face. His eyes reflected zero pity. How could he do this to me? And Mom, oh God, why was she here? Mom didn't do things like this. Her silent show of solidarity devastated me and erased any sense of safety I'd ever felt. I kept looking at her in disbelief. And I'd fought with all my heart not to upset Hilary. I felt so sad. So betrayed. So desperate. And entirely alone.

Of course, I couldn't guarantee best behavior, but I didn't know what I'd do if I was left behind. I'd go mad. What if one of these times I can't find my way out? Will I be stuck in there forever?

At that moment, I realized there was no other option, so I looked my Dad in the eye and simply said, "I'll be fine. I promise. I can go."

Chapter IV
Week Three: The Blonde "Raya Mer"

Date: Monday, October 17th
    Wall Street lunch, 12:00pm – 2:00pm
    West Village street time, 2:00pm – 5:00pm
    West Village happy hour, 5:00pm – approx 8:00pm

* * *

Something had to be done with the blonde wig. The color appeared somewhat natural online, but what I got was Jessica Simpson platinum. I looked... stupid.

After a dye job from Agent Thorn, the hue was now more golden than white, but as the wig dried, it puffed up into a lion's mane with split ends. To make it less immense, I pulled some strands back and went with an ethereal look: Think sixties, flower-child style but with enough hair for three hippy chicks. It wasn't like the others. As a scientist, this loss of experimental control made me sigh.

Thorn and I met in front of the stock exchange. It was a bright, sunny day. I felt fake. And fluffy. My first glance in a dark window gave me a nasty shock —I was all hair and a startlingly bright mass of it at that. I was too engrossed in figuring out what I looked like to pay much attention to anyone else trying to answer the same question, although I did quickly observe that the hostile, *persona non grata* vibe that greeted me last week, as Nada, was absent.

Agent Thorn mentioned that most of the looks conveyed the idea that I must've strayed into this area by mistake. After a dozen blinding window reflections, I declared myself an unnatural disaster. Hopefully, I just had a bad case of wig change/color shock, and my eyes only needed time to adjust to the light, but I doubted that.

We passed an unmoving line that snaked along several blocks. To our astonishment, we discovered they were all waiting for free Bon Jovi tickets. Despite their questionable taste in music, we saw this as a good research opportunity and walked alongside the line for a bit. Most people were busy in their own world, but Thorn did have some stats to report.

20 looks from men
10 from women
bitchy glares from 2 young women in line.

We ate lunch outdoors at a nice restaurant in Hanover Square. The waitress wasn't friendly with me and acted put out that she had to serve us. She wasn't outrageously rude or suspicious like the hostess last week, but I got the message that my appearance didn't please her.

Afterwards, we set out to vagabond around the West Village for the afternoon.

"I feel so odd. Forest Gump, Fairy circles, 4-H county fairs, and patchouli are coming to mind. And I feel like I should have green gardening clogs on."

Agent Thorn agreed.

I found I felt my prettiest when surrounded by shrubs and other greenery.

After frequenting a couple of coffee stops, we picked an outdoor café for our pre-un-happy hour drinks. A handsome man, with an irresistible Irish brogue, winked at me when I went inside. Then, as I waited for the ladies' room to become available, our waiter insisted that I use the men's, so I wouldn't have to wait further. I counted this as high flattery and started feeling a tad sexy.

As an entertainment bonus, Lauren Hutton sat at a table near us. She wore garishly colored, hideous sneakers with an eggshell colored pantsuit. From the ankles up, Lauren was lovely.

Street time in West Village:
1 man w/ stroller
1 bicycle guy
1 30s guy in car
7 assorted 30s–40s men passing by
1 raised eyebrow from guy with tons of hair
1 older woman with possible wig gave friendly look
1 girl with crazy hair
1 model type blond
1 older, silver-haired Irish man inside cafe
1 hot-looking 30s guy
1 displeased woman
1 scruffy 30s guy who looked like he thought he knew you
1 Really Bitchy Look by woman behind us

We moved on to our old haunt, the White Horse Tavern. We sat in our usual place, and the same young guy was our server. He didn't care enough to recognize us. The usual handful of older men were stationed at the bar, a group of girls gossiped in a corner, and a few couples and tourists passed through. Agent Thorn and I settled in with our beers and resumed one of our staple conversations.

"An affair is out of the question." Thorn laughed at me. "You have a terrible lying face and besides, you can't keep anything to yourself. You'd confess instantly."

"I know. And I have no control over that face either. Even if I think about lying, I feel my eyes widening. But things are getting more complicated. This experiment has opened Pandora's box. I'm more confident now. And we're having a wacky, fun adventure. I don't want to give up this energy.

But what if I turn back into a hermit who does crosswords in bed?"

"No way. You know you can handle going out and having a nightlife just fine now."

"But I can't just break up with Tim and think everything is going to be ok. It's thanks to him that I've managed to stay out of "mental spas" since I came to New York City. But this going out, dressing up, and looking at men is making me wild! Say, what do you think about garter belts? I've always thought they were sexy, but it never occurred to me to wear one. The last few days, I've become increasingly fascinated with them."

"You mean you've never worn one? Seriously?" Thorn was sincerely shocked. "Well, they're tons of fun. They're great for play but not every day. But yeah, they're fabulous. I parade around in sex outfits for my boyfriend all the time."

"Really? I've never even worn thigh-highs. It's not fair. I want to parade around in sex outfits all the time, too."

"Go out and buy some; it's as easy as that."

"But who am I going to wear it for?"

"Can't you try it with Tim?"

"I guess I can, but I don't really want to. It won't be exciting to go pick them out if I think of him either. I'm already turned off."

After a couple of beers, we called it a night. A doomed yet thrilling feeling told me that I'd started something I couldn't stop.

* * *

Date: Tuesday, October 18th
Fields of Research:
    Chinatown to Soho morning walk, 11:30 am – noon
    Soho Starbucks/street time, noon – 2:00 pm

Open Center 2:00 pm   6pm
Soho Dinner and Bar frequenting, 6:00 pm – 11:00 pm

* * *

The day started off with the discovery I was out of clean underwear. I'd bought more than a dozen pairs of official project panties, but I'd had no time to mess with laundry, so I had a judgment call to make. In the end, I decided it was better to go *au naturel* than to destabilize the experiment by wearing rogue undergarments. Besides, today I had on jeans, and Raya was a hippie. I'd buy more project panties in the afternoon.

It was another beautiful, sunny day. As I walked up Mott Street, making my way from Chinatown to Soho, every man, woman, and chicken looked at me. Finally, I'd managed to steal people's attention. In fifteen minutes, I counted more than forty looks. Mostly, I startled people and made old women flinch. My eyes instinctively wanted to lower themselves in apology, but I forced myself to meet people's gazes, and I banned the self-torture of glancing into dark windows. Being a giant, frizzy Barbie pained me. Plus, my ass hurt for some reason, and everything pissed me off.

When I walked into Starbucks, I spotted Kermit sitting in his usual spot. He looked up briefly, but I couldn't read him. He only fancied me as a redhead, I guess. During our hour and a half stay, Thorn reported about a dozen guys and two women took notice, one of whom was fair-haired and gazed upon me snobbishly. On our way out, I suggested we call this wig, The Blonde Bomb.

Our short street time stroll revolved around my wish to find a hat, but nothing cute would fit on my head.

As soon as I walked through the Open Center door, the receptionist threw her hands up in the air. "You are too much, too much girl. Morticia is gone, and now here comes the mermaid!"

If I couldn't be a blonde bombshell, mermaid sounded fine. I thought back to an afternoon I had spent on a small boat in the Pacific, years ago. I had laid my head on the side of the boat and looked down at the jellyfish floating in the still, blue water. A stingray glided through the water below, and the beauty was almost too much to survive.

That's how I wanted to feel: alive in the moment and at peace. No thoughts, just wonder. Suddenly, I knew my blonde name: Raya Mer.

Raya de Mar is *stingray* in Spanish. I made a little change for her last name and used Mer instead of Mar because I thought it sounded better, and I felt like throwing a French word in there to remind people that my new alter ego was no dumb blonde.

Otto offered up a bright side to my wild hairdo. "You know, because it's bushy and appears to be a tad abused, it almost looks the most real because it's not so perfect and shiny."

Then, just for fun, I showed him some pictures I took right after I'd taken the wig off at the end of a day and night's tour of duty.

"Oh, she's cute. So, is that your accomplice?"

"Huh?"

"Her, who's she?" And he pointed to my photo.

"No, that's me you idiot." I grabbed the camera back from him and double-checked. "Jesus, Otto, that's me."

This information sent waves of glee through him. "Oh, I've forgotten what you look like!"

Later, we snuck off and did a little photo shoot in one of the Center's event rooms. Otto even set up fans for a couple of windswept shots. He urged me to make love to the camera and work it harder. His fussing over me boosted my confidence, and my sides hurt from laughing so hard. Then the pictures stunned me. I looked so different, and I thought maybe even beautiful in a few of them.

The images also revealed the need for me go purchase underwear immediately since I had a lovely case of camel toe. While at Victoria's Secret, I picked up twenty more pairs of project panties, a bunch of fishnet stockings and two French burlesque dancer outfits, complete with bustier, panties, and garters. When I got back to the office, I spread out my purchases in front of Otto.

"Look, my first sex outfits! As I walked back here, I felt like I was a sex super-hero and had secret weapons in my bag. I got the fishnets, the garters, everything. Now, I just need bedroom shoes."

"Very sexy, very French. So, now what are you going to do with it? I mean you and your boyfriend don't even screw anymore, right?" Otto looked at me with arched eyebrows.

"Um. Right. I haven't figured that out yet. Damn it, Otto, I want a monster of a man!"

"Oh, girl, you're in trouble."

* * *

Agent Thorn and I met for an early dinner and then headed into the Soho nightlife. We drank Cosmopolitans at a chic bar and talked about why on earth six life-sized, rhinestone panthers were mounted high up on the thirty-foot wall. The glittering kitties were frozen in various predatory poses, each one trapped inside its very own glass cube. I could relate to how odd they must've felt because I also felt frozen and out of place until our Cosmos kicked in.

On the way to our next stop, we passed a lingerie boutique called Agent Provocateur. In the storefront window, two mannequins were dressed up in black S&M-inspired outfits. They were upside down, suspended in mid-air, and in the middle of performing an erotic magic act. We took a field snapshot of me standing next to the ladies. I felt very clothed next to them.

"Should I unbutton my shirt a couple of notches so I don't look so prudish?"

"YES, YES, YES!" A young, jock-type guy shouted as he walked by with his girlfriend. She gave him a death look, but he kept yelling.

An older man was out in the street, directly in front of the window, busy setting up his camera. He peered through the lens, fussed with the settings, and didn't pay us any mind, but I still felt silly posing in his presence. At first, I thought he must be lecherous and creepy to go to so much trouble to take this shot, but then I remembered this was Manhattan, and it wasn't strange. He then paused with his work and good-naturedly took pictures of Thorn and me together.

Thorn and I went back to the Irish bar we'd visited during both Kali's and Nada's weeks. The same bartender who chatted me up as a redhead was now chatting up Agent Thorn. Instantly, I was dejected and felt personally rejected. My hundredth mood swing for the day was just ninety-eight too many. It frustrated me that for all my genuine effort, the around the clock inner therapy sessions and positive self-talk, here I was emotionally crushed *again. Why the hell do I care what a bartender thinks about me? I don't want to care.* I wore myself out.

The pink Victoria's Secret bag sitting on the floor next to my barstool caught my attention. I'd forgotten all about my new lingerie! A delicious surge of excitement pulsed through me, and I frowned at the feeling.

Is this an okay level of excited? Is this a normal amount of lustful longing? Is it long overdue fun or the start of something dangerous? It pissed me off that I had to step in, like a sour recess monitor telling kids not to play on the jungle gym.

"You know, an increasingly out-of-control libido is a big sign of a manic up-swing. I *think* it's normal that I'm feeling it more because I'm actually going out, and all this dressing up and new girly stuff is lots of fun."

Agent Thorn paused and looked pensive. "Well, I think it is normal. You don't have a sex life with your boyfriend. You're finally doing things you never thought you could do. You should be able to have fun."

"Yeah, I think it's natural, too. I'm not out of control, at all. And I want to be able to have fun."

* * *

Tim knew all about my insatiable, manic sexual appetite. Thanks to it, we'd had oodles of mad, crazy, oh-wow sex in our time. Sex was actually pretty hot for quite a while, but I couldn't imagine any kind of rekindling now. I always had to bring all of the passion; he never started anything.

It didn't bother me so much when I was depressed because what he lacked in the take-charge department he more than made up with compassion and comfort, but his passiveness angered me when I wasn't weak and needy. During manic highs, when I was invincible and erotically super-charged, I resented him for it. And I resented myself for being so screwed up that I had to depend on him. I never cheated, and I felt guilty about thinking he was a big pussy. I tried not to show it, but it showed.

Really, I was the one who killed our sex life. I did it by breaking up with him this last winter during a manic upswing. After I crashed down from my high a short time later, I came crawling back, a depressed, hysterical mess, and begged him to take me back. He rejected me at first but finally relented. When he finally did, it was out of a sense of duty. Basically, we both knew he was coming back only because I couldn't survive without him. It was a sacrifice on his part. He nursed me through that agonizing summer of depression, and now I was back on my feet. And back to resenting him. And myself. The new ingredient in this old recipe was Tim: He was now resenting me back.

It was after ten when I got home from the bar. I wanted to crash, but I still had another mission to accomplish. Something had to be done with the wig. It was too wild, and for the sake of research, I wanted it to look more like the others. Thorn didn't have time to come over and condition it, and I didn't dare trust myself because the one wig I'd washed in the sink came out permanently dreadlocked. I couldn't risk destroying our only blond wig. Finally, I came up with the idea of showering with it on and washing it like it was my own hair. Thorn and I didn't see any reason why it wouldn't work but now, after wearing it all day, it was the last thing I wanted to do.

After procrastinating for two hours, I stood in the shower, naked under the hot water, as someone else's wet hair trailed down over my breasts and hung heavily down my back and arms. This has gone too far. This was wacky. While I combed a bottle of conditioner through it, I wondered to whom this hair had belonged and what her life was like. Although, after thinking about it, surely this mane came from more than one person. How many other women were in the shower with me? Suddenly, everything felt far too intimate, far too personal. It was unsettling but also very sensual. The heavy sensation of thick, wet strands on my skin delighted me, and I enjoyed the sight of tendrils clinging to my body. Combing it gave me great pleasure, and I pretended it was all mine. Then I snapped out of it and felt creepy.

* * *

I made Tim take a very weird shower with me once at his apartment. It was the middle of the night when I dragged him into the bathroom and asked him to get in with me.

"Why now?"

"Please just get in. Come on. Please, it's important."

He mumbled something and shook his head. I pulled him in anyway.

We were naked, pressed together under the stream of hot water while I told him about my secret chemistry experiment. "Seriously, it can save the world, but only if you pee in the shower with me!"

"What are you talking about? Jesus, Stacy. I'm not gonna pee in the shower with you. No way." He looked so funny. His eyes had widened in disbelief, and now he was blinking fast and squinting as the water pelted his shocked face. We giggled until our knees buckled.

"Stop. I'm serious." I regained my sense of mission. "If there's even the slightest glimmer that you believe me, please do it. Or even if you don't believe me, please, it's just pee!" I pleaded with him on behalf of all existence.

Truly, I believed that in some cosmic and mysterious way, the combination of our pee and body sloughings going down the drain would find their way into the mystic elixir and be the final strands of DNA needed to complete the magic formula that would bring forth Utopia. At the time, I could have told you, in great detail, exactly what this meant and why it made sense. I suppose, if I thought about it really hard, I could retrieve some of that reasoning, but then it was a huge, otherworldly concept that reached to infinity and spun around on waves of superhuman reckoning. My regular brain can't do it justice.

"First," he said, "let me make this clear. I don't believe you. And, I need you to understand that I'm only going to pee in the shower for you this once, got it? Once. Jesus, Stacy."

I jumped up and down in joy and kissed him. He didn't have to believe because I knew it was true.

"Thank you! Ok, now hold onto the curtain rod and make sure your toes are touching the metal part of the drain, too."

"Christ. I can't believe I'm doing this. Never again."

Then we did it.

I figured my part was now done and the universe would sort out how to use our genetic material and take care of all the salvation work. Euphoria and ecstasy washed over me.

This little anecdote isn't a horrifying one for me at all. "I'm only peeing in the shower once," is a big inside joke between Tim and me. So, when I told Agent Thorn the story, her reaction surprised me: She didn't laugh.

"Well, I guess it is funny, and it is weird, sure, but it's more disturbing than anything. Why did he go along with it? Obviously, you were off your rocker. Did he do anything about it? Did he call your doctor at least?"

Good questions. And I honestly don't remember. Chronological and linear memories sometimes just don't exist. I don't think he did do anything, actually. Which may be shocking from the outside, but this was just one example from one night. To be sure, he had times when he took action, but when this is the norm in your life, I guess normal rules don't apply.

I had been telling Thorn that no other man could roll with my "eccentricities" the way Tim did. I'd used this incident as an example of how Tim always stuck by me no matter how weird things got. He was what kept me safe and out of hospitals. Now I can see how precariously off the rocker our little life together was, but I guess my focus was on the miraculous fact that he never ran away.

* * *

Date: Wednesday, October 19th
Fields of Research:
   Midtown power business lunch, noon – 1:00pm
   Midtown to Upper West Side street time, 1:00pm – 2:30pm
   Upper West Side loitering, 2:30pm – 4:00pm
   Wild Card Night with Steve 7:00 pm - late

* * *

My power lunch venue choice wasn't doing it for me. I peered in through the windows and could see the restaurant was half-empty and very dark. So, I waited for Thorn outside. In the meantime, a steady stream of businessmen walked past and every one took a good look at me. That made me wonder what was wrong.

I spied a reflective background behind the apples at the corner fruit stand, so I went over to check that everything was where it should be. It was, and I thought my blonde hair looked great now. It was a hell of a lot tamer. Even smooth. Surely, some of these men had to be lusting after me. While I paced around the sidewalk, I fancied they were wondering which model or star they'd just sighted.

Agent Thorn arrived and agreed we should go somewhere else. She suggested the big-shot lunch scene at Café Central, which was inside Grand Central. We decided to walk over.

"While I was waiting for you I racked up the stare stats! I think conditioning it did the trick."

"Oh, yeah, it's definitely more in control, but it's still a hell of a lot of hair. I still think the surprise factor is the big reason for the stares."

She kicked me off my star in one breath! But if my appearance was so surprising, and the attention had nothing to do with attraction, then why were so many men but hardly any women noticing me?

The young hostesses stationed at Cafe Central's entrance podium welcomed us coldly. Their expressions conveyed what they were thinking: *You're a hussy and not worthy of our attention.* I smirked in return and hoped they got my message: *Please ladies, don't cast stones, y'all are wearing black, spandex booty pants. Now lead us to our table.* Finally, one of them picked up two menus with a huffy sigh and motioned for us to follow.

Café Central was huge, and the numerous tables were filled with mostly well-dressed businessmen along with a few businesswomen. I'd say we were the only people under fifty there for social reasons. A handful of men, including waiters and busboys, were especially attentive to what was going on near our table, but the women didn't even glance in my direction.

Our seat was in a sunny spot, right next to the floor-to-ceiling windows, and the natural light made me twitchy. The bright light and the ego ache caused by Thorn's "blonde shock factor" theory set me up to believe I was a head-turning hay bale. I itched inside my own skin. I had to find a way to reclaim my dignity.

On my way to the bathroom, I passed a large table full of businessmen and one very attractive and dynamic, blonde businesswoman. She was addressing everyone at the table in a professional, businesslike tone when half of the men broke their attention to look my way. She continued speaking without acknowledging their distraction or the source of it. I was impressed. It's a small thing, but in a professional, male dominated scenario like this, I think how well a woman handles rude, testosterone moments is subtly important.

Later, as we put in Upper West Side street time, I realized that I really hated wearing black this week and longed to be wearing earth tones and flowing skirts. Surely, warmer colors would help me blend and feel better. Meanwhile, I wished Thorn would quit saying I looked like a bimbo.

Since Steve and I were going out to do some wildcard research later that evening, Thorn and I altered our plan and went shopping for a colorful outfit for me to wear. As soon as I put on a dress, which was green with earthy brown accents, snug fitting, wonderfully textured and charming in a French bordello way, I felt as natural as foliage. I bought it immediately.

When we left the boutique, we passed Conan O'Brien, who was engaged in a vigorous conversation with another guy. He didn't look.

Next, I had to go face my therapist. I sat down on the couch, and she leveled me with a long, hard look.

"I see it's poofier than the others."

I changed the subject. "I don't know what to do about Tim. It's dire this time!"

My therapist laughed, settled back in her chair and took in a deep breath, "Stacy, I remember sitting here listening to the same thing around this time last year. Do you recall what happened then?"

I didn't have to answer that.

"You broke up with him, and after a couple of months, you were a distraught mess and came crawling back. You decided you couldn't live without the stability he gave you and decided to stay put. What makes you think it'll be different this time?"

"That's the problem. I don't. But I know there's no way he'd take me back this time."

"Well, this is nothing new. It's the age-old dilemma between balancing security and passion: the whole scenario of a man with a wife and then the mistress. You don't want to do that, do you?"

"No. It's not fair to keep him around just to take care of me either. And it doesn't feel fair to me that I can't fucking take care of myself. I don't know what to do."

"It's not a healthy situation for either of you, but we don't want another botched break-up job. You're not ready."

After that uncomfortable brush with reality, my next order of business was meeting up with Steve. He gave me a hello kiss on the cheek and exclaimed, "Wow. You're white hot and that dress is freaking off the hook."

Ah, just what I needed.

We passed a Rasta guy hanging out with a couple of dreadlocked dudes outside a nameless club. He started performing a mute, ride-the-pony/stir-the-soup dance. As we walked past, he kept on riding and stirring and smiling without a word.

"What on earth was that?"

"I have no idea, but it was all for you my dear."

"Cool!" Bring it on. Lavish me with attention.

Spice Market, an enormous and cavernous Moroccan restaurant in the uber-trendy Meatpacking District, was our first stop. We were lucky to nab seats at the bar. Thorn and I had a cocktail here last week, and the same surfer boy bartender who'd served me without ado as Nada now handed me my drink with a wink.

A pretty, blonde woman sat next to me at the bar, and her date stood hovering near my shoulder.

"Don't you dare look at that floozy," a *ssss* sound whistled through her teeth at the end, like a venomous, snake hiss.

"Steve, did you hear that? She just called me a *floozy*."

"Yeah, I did. That's brutal. Man, I was watching another poor guy with a girl at the bar, and he was just itching to look. I thought, *oh buddy no, no, don't*. And then, why'd you do that, you idiot, and she was talking to you—at least be a little more subtle."

I flirted heavily and teased Steve with tales of my wild, sexual romps of yore. I also told him how much I appreciated some good old male aggression in the bedroom. When I confessed that my current sex life was dead, he appeared perplexed.

"Dude, you're in quite a pickle, and your horniness is totally off the hook. I don't know what to tell you."

* * *

Date: Thursday, October 20th
Fields of Research:
    Home 8:00 pm – late

* * *

Agent Thorn and I knocked off early that Thursday, and I decided to make an effort to spend time with Tim. I even drummed up enough desire to surprise him with my new lingerie. He was still working when I called and very reluctant to come over, but I persuaded him with the promise of a special treat.

Left with an hour to prepare, I commanded myself to quit whining. I needed to go into this with gusto and let my sex hungry body go wild. Besides, as a couple, we both deserved an honest effort. So, by the time Tim arrived, candles were flickering, music was playing, and my surprise was waiting for him underneath my new, green dress.

I greeted him with a kiss and then stepped back and held my arms out for his viewing pleasure and performed a seductive *ta-da*. Tim nodded absently, sat down at my table, and began checking his email.

"Ugh, don't you like my outfit? Haven't you noticed the romantic mood I'm trying to create? Look at all the candles."

I knew he wasn't thrilled that I was wearing a wig. He didn't like feeling the wigs against his skin at all. He found them creepy and said he felt he was being swatted by a horse's tail. My hair was a sweaty mess underneath, and I hadn't taken the time to shower. I decided to spend the time lighting candles and putting on lingerie. Maybe he just couldn't face having to touch my fake hair, but he could get over it!

"Yeah, it's great. I'll just be a minute." His tone was flat, and his eyes were glued to his hotmail account.

That disgusted me, but I wasn't going to quit, so I started moving languidly to the music and touched his shoulder.

"I want you to undress me. Please." He looked confused but finished up his email and followed me. I pulled him close and swayed slowly. Tentatively, he pulled off enough of my dress to reveal the tops of the garters and stockings.

"Wow..." He was lost in wonder for a moment, like a kid marveling at the hidden treasure he'd just uncovered. His hands ran over my body, stopping to play with the bustier and pull on the garters. Then, suddenly, he stopped and retreated to my bed. He stripped off his clothes, jumped under the covers, and waited. I stood half-naked in the middle of the room and watched him pull the sheets up to his chin.

"Hey, what are you doing? Come back! I wanted to do a little strip tease dance for you. I want to show you my whole outfit. It's new lingerie. I've never worn garters. Please." I begged.

"But I'm already under the covers."

"Please." I stomped my feet and begged some more. He finally got up.

It all ended less than ten minutes later with me sitting up naked in bed, unzipping my leather boots and flinging them off in a huff. I sat fuming. This meek and sweet crap was disgusting me, and I just couldn't hide it.

"You know, a girl needs some passion, and this is just sad."

Tim *looked* sad, but agreed and was understanding. It killed me to see him like this, but I also wanted to kill him for it.

I apologized and took some of the blame. After all, he's not stupid, and I couldn't expect him to leap into action at the snap of my icy fingers.

"It's ok; no big deal," and then we kissed and joked around like buddies. Once he was asleep, I curled up and cried.

* * *

Date: Friday, October 21st
Fields of Research:
    Metropolitan Museum of Art 5:00 pm – 7:00 pm
    Hell's Kitchen 7 pm – late

* * *

We chose the rooftop terrace bar at the Metropolitan Museum of Art for our upscale happy hour. Friday nights were especially popular there for welcoming in the weekend with a cultured drink. It also had the reputation for being an upscale pick-up place. The terrace was huge with plenty of space for mingling and people watching, as well as unlimited access to an amazing view of Central Park and the city. Single women could lean on the railing and gaze into the horizon for a long time, giving men an available signal. Well, that's what I planned on doing anyway. So when we arrived at the museum and the guard told us the terrace had just closed for the season, I was bereft.

The Met had an exhibit of nineteenth-century Spirit Photography Thorn and I wanted to check out, and we decided to stop first in the cafeteria for a snack. I gravitated toward the dessert display where everything looked all too good.

A middle-aged man, who had a lost and lonely air about him, hovered next to me.

As I circled the goodies, I recognized he was looking at me in the same way I was looking at the cakes.

"You should get the Black Eyed Susan cupcake, just so I can see you get it."

"Oh no, it looks too decadent."

After giving me an overt up and down perusal he offered, "Oh, you look like you can handle decadent just fine to me."

"Well, yes *I* can, but I don't know about my waist."

"You're breaking my heart."

He made me crave the chocolate sin, but I took the carrot cake with cream cheese icing instead because of idiotic dietary reasoning.

Thorn and I sat at one of the tables in the back. I picked at my cake and ate it without joy.

"Why the hell didn't I just get the chocolate one? After last night, I deserve any kind of sinful pleasure I can get my hands on."

"Why, what happened?"

"Oh God. The lingerie. It was awful. I don't even want to tell you."

"You wore it for Tim?"

"Yeah, and he ran away from me. He hid under the covers."

"You're kidding me! What is wrong with him? Is he gay? That's not normal."

"I don't know. He acted like a timid, little boy. I mean at one point he actually hid behind a door. He was scared of me."

"What? This makes no sense. Did you even get to have sex?"

"Maybe for five minutes. I was in garters and fishnets, and all he wanted to do was cuddle. I blew up and yelled at him. I'm so depressed." I stared at my cake. "He agreed it was pathetic, and we talked about it, but you should have seen his face. He was so sad. So, I apologized, and we joked around. And honestly, it's not his fault. He's not stupid. He knows I'm not happy and probably thinks there's nothing he could do to please me. That's a libido killer. And then, I just show up in lingerie on a chance night off and demand him to perform. That's not fair."

"Fair or not, I don't care, the dude is not normal. Trust me."

"No, no, it's not so simple. I mean he was my caretaker for most of the year when I was depressed; he didn't even want to get back together with me but did because I needed help, and now I'm off running around and getting all sexed up, without him. He's a good guy, but I can't stand it. And even before this, I always had to bring the spark to start things. I want a man who goes crazy with desire for me."

By the time we left, I felt even more miserable. As I walked out the cafeteria door, I heard Thorn gasp.

"Stacy, Stop!" I turned around and saw a face full of horror and confusion. "It's your wig. The infrastructure is showing. I can see the basket-weave mesh shining against the white wig cap."

"No, that can't be! You never saw it before did you?"

We stood at the base of the stairs, frozen and in shock.

"It couldn't have been there since I've spent so much time staring at the back of your head, but now that I see it, it's obvious."

"But this is Friday. You would've seen it by now. Maybe it's the lighting? Is it that bad?"

"Oh, it's *really* bad I'm afraid. I'm sorry, but it is. Maybe it is just a lighting fluke. It is ultra-florescent and bright here."

We walked towards the Spirit Photography exhibit with Thorn trailing behind me.

All I heard from Thorn were gasps and giggles, "I can still see it. I know it's not funny, but it *is*, and I don't think it's the lighting."

It was bad, but it wasn't bad enough to keep us from the Spirit photos.

The display of old black and white photographs featuring haunted puffs of smoke, shadowy ghosts and supernatural ectoplasm was very cool, but I couldn't really relax. I swear the back of my scalp was blushing. How humiliating to be caught wearing a badly constructed wig in one of the most respected art museums in the world.

A young, preppy couple recoiled from me in shock, and I observed how the smiles and flirty looks from a handsome man turned into expressions of bewilderment. Soon, Thorn pulled me into a corner and reported an old woman had been pointing my head out to her husband.

"We have to abort and go fix it."

We rushed to a bathroom, and Thorn handed me her compact so I could see for myself. I could see it plainly: a white and gold checkerboard. Did the wig develop alopecia overnight? Oh Lord, had it been like this the entire time? Surely, Otto, someone, would've noticed. And how could Thorn have missed it?

All the times I'd felt sexy over the last week now felt like a joke. Like when I was at dinner with Steve and a table full of great-looking men couldn't take their eyes off me and conferred animatedly when I passed by: had they been mesmerized or mocking me? Finally, Thorn managed to conceal the enormous blunder by pinning more of my hair back and artfully braiding over it.

Once we were back on the street, I'd struggled to gain a slight sense of humor but still felt shaken. "I'm scarred by this."

"Of course you are. I completely understand."

Oh no, Thorn wasn't supposed to agree. That flung me back into a tizzy.

* * *

Since our high-class cocktail plan wasn't happening, we opted for trying out the younger Hell's Kitchen crowd. We walked down a street packed with options and randomly picked a place called Joshua Tree. It was big and appeared to be a normal enough pub. Dining tables were on the second floor, but the hostess passed by the stairs and led us into a hidden, back room. What I saw in there confused me. We were descending into a deep, boxy pit with walls that were lined with an unending and enormous black, leather sectional. About thirty people shared this gigantic, sunken-in living room with us and the crowd was Very Young and Very Drunk. The lights were bright, and everyone was eating burgers the size of their own heads.

When Agent Thorn left for the bathroom, a trashed young man sitting on the couch next to me scooched over and slapped his hands on my thighs.

"Hey, you're so pretty," he said as he rubbed my legs. "My name's Ron. Hey, what are you eating? So, I'm Ron, who are you?" He was kind of geeky and harmless, so I took his hands and placed them on his own thighs without yelling at him.

"I'm getting the salad, and I'm Stacy."

"Nooo. Bad choice. Just look at those crazy onion rings over there, and the burgers—the burgers are insane." His hands made a big circle to illustrate their girth but then he suddenly looked at me in alarm. "You're gonna drink though, right? You're so pretty. I'm Ron." He laid his head on my shoulder for a moment, then snapped up, happily scooted away, and forgot about me.

"Bless you, Drunk Ron!" I called after him. He was the first guy to ask my name during this whole thing. After thousands of anonymous stares, I was relieved someone finally asked. And he said I was pretty. I was sure he'd be hitting on mailboxes within the hour, but he cheered me up.

After dinner, we were back outside, hunting for another

bar. A dude wearing a blinding amount of bling stopped me.

"Hey, now aren't you a pretty thing! What's your name?" We were in the middle of a crowded sidewalk, but he took hold of my hand, stretched out my arm, and then stepped back to get a full intake of my goods. "DA-YAAA-YUM!"

He warned me I wouldn't find another gem like him in the entire city. As he explained why I shouldn't let him get away, I counted at least ten jewels on his fingers, four layers of glittery necklaces and three rhinestone buckles. "Come with me to an all 'in people' party. Girl, you deserve to be there; it's the hottest thing in town." This made me feel giddy even though it was all bullshit.

I had to decline, but HOT DA-YAAA-YUM. He asked my name!

* * *

Date: Saturday, October 22nd
Fields of Research:

Union Square Afternoon street time/wandering around, 2:00pm – 5:00pm

Lower East Side late night bar scene, 10:00pm – early am

* * *

Dressed in my puffy leisurewear, I installed myself in the Union Square Barnes & Noble for a little book browsing. While I was perusing selections at the Odd & Humorous Table, I noticed the guy next to me was acting weird. He invaded my personal space, and he held one book in his hand without turning it over to read the back for too long. I felt something was off. A moment later, he tapped me on the shoulder.

"Hey, I like your outfit. It's wonderful. You know why?"

"No. Tell me because I have no idea," I said, vaguely amused.

He shifted around and then lowered his voice so he could lean in even closer, "Well, it gives you the *illusion* that you like to take care of your body, keep fit. It works very well."

His word choice irked me, so I took a better look at the guy to see if he had any room to talk. He had a big head, wore little glasses, and was probably in his late twenties. Additionally, he was short, stocky, had a huge ass, and his khaki pants were all bunched up around his crotch. His shifting around turned into more of a gross-looking squirm, and my creep alarm bells went off.

"My name is Alex. What's yours? I'd really like to get to know you. I can tell you're interesting. You're more than what you look like. I bet you're artistic. Tell me your name."

I kept flipping through books and didn't look at him. As soon as I'd move to put a few feet in between us, he closed right back in. This normally would've been my cue to leave, but I stuck around. "I'm Stacy, but I'm not that interesting."

He assured me, in a rush of whispers, that I was special and that he wanted to be my friend. Then, suddenly, he was panting.

"But I still would like to find out what makes your heart beat passionately, what makes it beat so hard that it feels like it is about to burst." He rubbed his groin against the table and closed his eyes. "Agghhh."

"Jesus, that's really sick!" I threw my book down and fled.

That's it, no more humoring perverts for the sake of experimental data! But, come on, that's not really why, is it? I made myself admit my real reason and let it sink in that I did it because I was feeling lonesome and ugly and was more than happy to have some sicko come stroke my ego. When he said that stuff about me being more than what meets the eye, it was like this gigantic maw of need opened. Maybe he could sense I was weak. I'd latch onto anything that made the maw feel better. But this was disgusting.

I marched myself out of the store and then straight through the park as if I were dragging some unruly child away to be punished. Then a dark window caught my attention, and I instinctively paused to look at myself. *STOP IT.* I crossed back over to the park and sat down on a bench. *I just let some creep masturbate next to me because he gave me a little attention. I let him do it. I even liked it. No more!*

Even though I was upset with my attention seeking, I was going to be paired up with my spare male spy tonight since Thorn wasn't available again.

Steve arrived, soaking wet, at my place around ten. We hung out and waited for the rain to pass. In the meantime, I showed him some photos of me in the different wigs. Most of them were field shots that Thorn had taken, but a few were from my own drunken, late night photo shoot. He oohed and ahhed at most of them but took a particular liking to one of me with blonde hair and a tripped-out, rainbow colored seahorse ornament dangling in front of my left eye.

"Wow, that's so killer-amazing, and the vibe is perfect for the blonde. Brilliant. You *have* to put this on *Hot or Not.*"

"What is that?" I yelled from the refrigerator as I fetched us two more beers.

"You mean you don't know? Just where have you been all these years, young lady? Give me your computer. We have to fix this now."

He showed me around the website, and I learned that here I could finally find out if I was indeed hot or not simply by posting my picture. Thousands of people would then rate me from one to ten, and I'd even get my own hotness percentage.

"But what if I score a two? How am I going to live with that?"

"I assure you; you'll get a nine or higher, don't worry."

No way in hell would I post a picture of the real me, but I figured one of my alter egos could handle a less than stellar rating. So, up Raya went to be judged.

* * *

By the time we hit the Lower East Side, both of us were happy and buzzed. We started off at Pianos, the same bar and live music venue that Thorn and I had visited the first week. After one drink downstairs at the crowded bar, I decided everyone was playing too nice. So, we went upstairs and hit the dance floor.

It was dark, packed, and loud up there. We squeezed past bodies until we were in the middle of the small but thumping scene. And, ooh, this dancing with long, blonde hair was good stuff. It gave me a whole new accessory to play with and incorporate into my choreography because I could even prance around it. This was a completely new experience of sensuality and allure.

Sweat rivers formed, and the itching started. That I could live with, since suffering for vanity was old hat by now, but I had another problem: My hair kept getting pulled this way and that by the constant contact with my fellow dancers. At first, I was worried, but I told myself to stay calm and above all not grab my head. Luckily, I managed to adjust things by creating a little dance flourish that included tugging on strands of hair on either side of my waist.

A large amount of grabbing and pelvic thrusting went on. Being a sought after part of this sweaty, gyrating tangle delighted me, however I'd shoo away the grinders after a quick minute and hang onto Steve.

But then he went M.I.A. during my first bathroom break. After ten minutes of searching, I gave up and stood in a corner. He must've gone home with some chick. How could he leave me here? Bastard.

Then, like magic, a little pathway parted amidst a sea of women, and there he was: smoothly rocking away with an ecstatic look on his face. I yanked him out of there.

"Stacy! You have no idea how cool it's been since you left. Don't take this the wrong way, but the entire time we were dancing together, I noticed all of these girls around us eyeing me. Like they really wanted me. They'd move in and out of our little circle to give me a little teasing rub and stuff behind your back, like they were trying to get away with something or even steal me. I thought I was just dreaming, but when you left for the bathroom, they all descended on me at once like a pack of rabid hotties."

"That's nice, but I thought you left me."

"Oh no, no way. But seriously, we're onto something here. This *never happens* to me."

We kept dancing. At one point, I shook it like Shakira and got a free drink.

Chapter V
Week Four: The Brunette, "Paula Isla"

The rich chestnut hue of my brunette wig was a lovely change from the meek and mousy shade of brown that I had been assigned by nature. I think Winston Churchill stepped out of line when he said, "I cannot pretend to feel impartial about colors. I rejoice with the brilliant ones and am genuinely sorry for the poor browns."

I didn't feel sorry for myself; I just wasn't sure how I felt. Perhaps it was due to this color not causing as much of a stir as the others, or maybe by this point in the experiment I was habituated to things that had previously impressed me. So, in search of an identity, I sought counsel from the wise men at Playboy. The introduction to "Playboy Brunettes," a photography book, reminded readers the Mona Lisa was a brunette.

"What she knows, every brunette knows. And not one has given it away." Readers were challenged to try and solve the mystery by studying the centerfolds within. "What does their silence tell you? Like the Mona Lisa, they prefer to let you wonder."

I came up with the brunette's moniker, Paula, because it seemed like a solid name and a good fit.

* * *

Date: Monday, October 24th
Fields of Research:
    Wall Street lunch, 12:00pm – 2:00pm
    West Village street time, 2:00pm – 5:00pm
    West Village happy hour, 5:00pm – approx 8:00pm

* * *

My outfit was still way off target for Wall Street but, coupled with a less alarming hair color, it wasn't enough to disturb the peace. Or maybe my tolerance had been built up.

Little looks no longer sent shivers down my spine. I told Thorn we needed to take a mini field trip to liven things up; somewhere with lots of people and action. We took off for Macy's.

On the subway there, a burly construction worker gave me long, approving looks. So, I was taken aback when Thorn reported he suddenly seemed to know something was amiss.

"His expression changed and then he kept scrutinizing you in disbelief. He totally knew, but I don't know why. I couldn't see anything wrong, so how on earth would this guy be the one to spot it?"

We decided he must work a bulldozer by day and a dress by night.

The one time in my life I actually wanted to be a part of Macy's mob scene, of course, coincided with the one time in history it was empty. Our exciting excursion was aborted.

As we walked back to the West Village, I felt off-kilter.

"I have sun spots. That's what I call it when I feel discombobulated and staticky in the brain. It can be scary sometimes because I can't think clearly, and then, if I panic, I end up a big, disoriented mess. So please don't let me walk into oncoming traffic."

Thorn knew most of my life story by now, so this didn't

surprise her. "Ok. I know what to do. We need to buy some beauty magazines, go to a café, and then mindlessly flip through them."

I laughed at her.

"I'm sorry, but that's the best thing I can think of!" Thorn continued, "It's good for checking your mind out, so maybe it will help. I find it strangely therapeutic."

These magazines usually annoyed me, but we got a couple and gave it a try.

Our experimental partnership, with all our banter and bickering, had turned us into a sort of half-ass comedy duo. We had fun with it and never truly got mad at each other. Beyond our regular shtick, I could talk about my past travails, including tales of mental wards, mania, and depression, as well as general chat about guys, relationships, and fun, girl stuff. Thorn was a generous listener, brought much needed perspective to subjects I'd never been able discuss at length before, filled me in on pop culture, and she was damn fun and funny. Life felt lighter and happier. We were becoming friends, and being inside my own skin was finally starting to feel ok. Just the fact that I could go out on the town every day and night with Thorn and not act totally batty did wonders for my confidence. This experiment that became an adventure was putting me through a social boot camp.

We settled into a café and started flipping through the glossy pages. I wasn't impressed. "How pathetic is this. They're saying *let your REAL YOU shine through* and *flaunt your uniqueness* but then they tick off twenty things you can't walk out the door in!"

Agent Thorn looked up from behind her magazine with a knowing smile and shook her head. "No. It doesn't work that way my friend. One doesn't question the mental health magazines. One just goes along!"

I had to admit my sunspots were receding.

* * *

We put in our West Village street time and reconfirmed our earlier findings. I guess I looked normal. Thorn only had one stat to report.

On street, 6:00 pm: 1 30s guy with glasses.

As soon as I got home after unhappy hour, I threw my wig and clothes on the floor, plopped down naked on my bed, and sought solace in the arms of the Internet. I checked my email with low hopes for anything interesting, but I found a surprise waiting for me.

"Raya, someone at Hot or Not wants to meet you!"

Inside were pictures of at least fifty men along with intro blurbs. Wow, Steve didn't tell me this was part of the ratings deal! I didn't see anyone that enticed me to investigate further, but an inbox full of pictures of men pleased me just enough to count as my excursion for the day.

* * *

Date: Tuesday, October 25th
Fields of Research:
    Open Center 2:00 pm – 6:00 pm
    Soho Dinner and Bar frequenting, 6:00 pm – 11:00 pm

* * *

When I arrived at the Open Center, Otto greeted me with a frowny face.

"Now that one just ain't grabbin' me," he said in a flat voice. "It's not as much fun as the others. Boring. Don't like it. Next!"

A guy from registration yelled across the hall and cut Otto off.

"No way! It's the best one because it works with her eyes! And look at her makeup; it's really nice today, too."

We decided that yes, my eyes and eyebrows really did blend in fabulously but meh, so do beige walls and loafers.

Otto's drop in enthusiasm level worried me. During the next couple of hours, my journal filled up with self-help pep talks:

Just let yourself be and let everything else fall where it will and don't waste time worrying if other people like me or not or custom tailoring myself to fit them. I'm OK

* * *

That evening Thorn and I went to Balthazar, a flashy French Bistro in Soho, for dinner.

1 40s waitress kind of stared
1 couple
1 40s guy looked.

So, everything was neutral, but we had fun. We drank vodka and talked about me having affairs.

"If you can manage it, hold off until the project is finished. Perhaps you can feed yourself on little flirtatious dalliances or something in the meantime."

"But what about my face? My eyes bug out, my forehead stretches, and my mouth freezes in a stupid smile if I even think of lying."

"Oh crap! I forgot about that. Affairs are out."

Our barhopping afterwards was pretty low-key. Here's the skinny.

The Ear Inn 8:45:
2 men in their 60s
1 30s man
1 waitress looked at you weird
1 smile from man

2 looks on way to bathroom
1 major look from bartender

* * *

Before I went to bed, I browsed through another batch of *Hot or Not* men. I'd almost reached the bottom of the pile when I was pulled up against the screen by strong, beautiful arms and kissed by the most sensual lips in existence. My God! Eyes like glowing black almonds, a face chiseled from God-man marble, and hands that required an evolution in the human language to describe. I clicked *Yes, I want to meet you.*

* * *

Date: Wednesday, October 26th
Fields of Research:
　　Midtown power business lunch, noon – 1:00pm
　　Midtown to Upper West Side street time, 1:00pm – 2:30pm
　　Upper West Side loitering, 2:30pm – 4:00pm
　　Wild Card Night with Steve 7:00 pm – late

* * *

I woke up, went straight to my computer to check my email, and there it was! The last line of his message, "*Shall we?*" made me dance around the room while I got ready to go out.

Then I was off to our power lunch at Asia de Cuba near Grand Central Station.

Billowy white panels of fabric flowed down from the high ceiling, diffusing warm, soothing light. Glass half-walls on the second floor added glints of silvery sheen and created a nice waterfall effect. An amazing community table—at least forty feet long—sat in the center of the first floor dining room.

Unfortunately, the power lunch scene lacked punch. Groups of well-dressed women, who I'd wager would be doing some serious after-lunch shopping, made up most of the clientele. Experiment-wise, the attention level followed the general theme of the week—nice and neutral.

While the good-looking waiter flirted and the guy who refilled our water gave us cheeky grins, I told Thorn all about my *Hot or Not* stallion.

"I've never been so affected by a mere photo in all my life. Of course I have to fall for a man's mind first, but I swear I could feel his energy…"

Thorn put her hand up. "Stop," she barked. "Oh my God. Are you listening to yourself? You can't be serious about some dude's picture from a website called *Hot or Not*! You can *feel his energy*? Please!"

Wow, I'd foolishly taken her nodding and the blank look on her face, as a sign she shared my amazement.

Thorn strangled her napkin.

"But you should see his eyes!" I gushed.

"Jesus H! You're not going to talk with him are you?"

"Well, why not?"

"He's not going to want to just chat. He's going to want to meet you and that's not all he'll want!"

Her violent eye rolling made me dizzy.

"I just want to see if there's anything there." I reasoned.

"Jesus, how can there be anything there, Stacy? Enough!"

We dropped it after I told her she was just too jaded, and she said something about me being too big of a moron.

On our way to the Upper West Side, I dragged Thorn into a Kinko's so I could go online and show her his picture. I knew that once she saw him, she'd understand it was kismet.

"Eww Yuck. No. No. No. Gross, what are you thinking?!"

"What do you mean? He's gorgeous! Look at his lips!" I leaned over the computer and looked into his face and then back at hers. I couldn't comprehend how she could be so wrong.

"Uh, no he's not. I'm not impressed; let's go."

As we logged street time, I got lectured on how a website like this was only about sex and hooking up, not soul mates. I wouldn't hear it, of course. Mysticism and love are found in the most unlikely places. Then I started to think about Tim. Just the other day, I'd written in my journal, with contrite conviction,

Cherish Tim. Make him feel loved. He's my best friend.

But now that changed to today's hurried scrawls.

Off-hinged. Tortured by passion, feel unsteady.

Agent Thorn's Notes

Grand Central area:

1 30s woman

2 young girls

1 morbidly obese man

1 UPS man

1 headphones guy

1 60s guy

Upper West Side streets:

2 40s men

1 30s woman gave you a mean look

1 older man

1 30s nanny

1 50s man

The afternoon wrapped up at a big, busy bakery. We took an interest in a middle-aged woman sitting near us who wore a puzzling, one-piece, black-velvet jumpsuit and had tons of very long, very crazy blonde hair. She alternated between writing frantically in her notebook and peering at us nervously. So, we wrote little notes back and forth trying to decide if she was doing an experiment of her own or was just a bit off. She seemed twitchy. We concluded that a fifty-year-old, post-breakdown Raya would look just like her.

I jotted down my diagnosis for her condition and scooted it over to Thorn. *New Age Celtic Part-Time Schizophrenic.*

We wanted to take her picture but figured it would freak her out. We were so awful, and yes, I know this gives me nary a right to moan and document all of the unfair and shallow judgments that have been bestowed upon *me* because of my hair or outfit. From the get-go, I was already aware that I was a hypocrite and a charlatan. Yet, perhaps it's only natural that after forty plus hours a week of observing gaggles of people, solely for the purpose of seeing if they were watching and passing verdicts on me, that our favorite pastime would become doing it back to a fair number of them.

Speaking of being a charlatan, it suddenly dawned on me that my new Internet love was writing to a woman with long, blond hair and blue eyes.

* * *

The experiment was lacking a gritty element, so I recruited Steve to do some extra nighttime recon with me at a dive bar.

Agent Thorn had suggested Rudy's Bar & Grill in Hell's Kitchen. "It has a big pig statue out in front of the place, and a lot of smashed people on the inside. The beer is really cheap, but no matter how drunk you get, don't eat the free hotdogs, and stay away from the floor. It's disgusting."

My first impression of Rudy's was that yes, you came here to get drunk. The bar was as long as the entire room, and it meant business. Wooden tables and benches lent to the overall barnyard air. It was a welcoming pigsty, though.

The place wasn't packed, but plenty of dudes were bellied up to the bar and drinking their weight in brew. Steve and I joined them and soon started talking with a guy we nicknamed Chip because he could've been Eric Estrada's twin. Chip became our friend after he heard us saying some stuff in Spanish.

"Oh, *mis amigos*. You speak *Español*. You guys are the REAL thing!" We assured him we weren't, but he insisted we were true Latinos in our *corazones*. Then he got a little sad. "I don't speak Spanish but *YO SOY PURA MEXICANA!*"

Overall, Chip was happy but did drop into moments of melancholia. "I love my wife. She is so beautiful, *mi* ángel, *mi vida*." He lowered his head and clasped his hands around his mug in a protective, tender gesture. "I just wish I could spend more time with her. I work so hard. It's the work, you know, and not the drink that keeps me away." Then he snapped his head up and started belting along to Bon Jovi's "Life is Like an Open Highway."

Chip leapt around striking rock star poses and playing air guitar in between buddy punching and joking with everyone.

When he came back, he looked at me and touched my hair. "You have witch's hair!"

I pulled away and started to protest.

"No, it's good," he yelled. "It's a really good thing. I wish my wife had witch's hair. It's sexy!"

"Why does it look like witch's hair?"

"It's the hairline." To my horror, he reached out traced it with his fingers. "Yes, yeah. True. You've got a great hairline."

I'd drunk a barrel of cheap beer, so I recklessly did a high-risk maneuver and flipped it around, "What about now?"

"It's wispy!" He was so pleased and gleeful. Then he howled and jumped up on the little stage to do his rock-star thing again.

The bartender, a stout, merry guy, bought us a round of drinks. A warm and dizzy state had already come over me, but this pint kicked it up several notches. I loved being slung over the bar with a beer in my hand and the smell of it all around. It gave me such a sense of happy camaraderie to be getting hammered along with everyone else. And Steve appeared very sexy in my low-lidded, slurry vision. I leaned in, and as my head whirled around pleasantly, I started kissing him. It was a perfect, slow motion, sloppy session that went on forever inside my killer buzz. It wasn't personal, though; I just wanted to kiss somebody.

We stopped and decided it could go no further. Then remorse set in.

Steve got serious. "You know, you're screwed if you decide to crucify yourself over this. You've got to square it away in your mind now. Right now. A little drunken kiss between friends isn't a sin."

I got home at 3:30 am. I know this because I found an email I'd sent to my *Hot-or-Not* guy at that hour. I believed it to be a work of staggering genius at the time that I sent it, but unfortunately, it translated into babble in the light of day.

* * *

Date: Thursday, October 27th
Fields of Research
    Cyber flirting, noon – 1pm
    Open Center, 2pm – 6pm
    Meatpacking District, 6pm – midnight

* * *

It was 11:30 am when I came to. I felt heavily damaged and smelled like a brewery. My sense of duty ordered me to get up, but it wasn't physically possible, so I called Thorn and cancelled our noon meeting. Instead of a stern talking-to, she reminded me that this was the first time we'd cancelled anything. It wasn't a problem. We'd just make it up.

"We've done remarkably well, actually." Thorn encouraged.

That relieved me from one of my guilty feelings. I pushed the other one, the kissing shame, out of my aching head.

Now I had time to recuperate before I went to the Open Center. And what better way than to make real-time contact with my fantasy man? Granted, adding another boy crime to my freshly committed one doesn't exactly follow reason, but I wasn't being reasonable.

My pulse fluttered as I typed in his IM address and wrote, "*Hello.*"

"*Hi! Great to hear from you! How much do you weigh?*"

"*What! You want to know my actual weight?*"

It seems he'd had some bad experiences so, yes, he wanted numbers.

"*You're being completely un-charming and maybe I'm not your type anyway. I have curves, and I'm not a waif. Bye.*"

"*I'm sorry. Wait! Please don't go. You don't have to tell me if you'll send a full body picture. Please. I want to talk to you.*" He went on to flatter and charm me, and I melted like butter. "*And thank you for your email, but it was in like three languages, and I didn't understand most of it.*"

"*You didn't even get the Romanian pick up line? I had a friend translate it just for you!*"

"*My Grandmother was Romanian, but I don't speak that much of it.*"

"*Ok. But why didn't you translate it?!*"

"*I would've but I've been busy filing motions for a case.*"

"*Well, I've already spent a night with you in my fantasies.*" This flew out of my fingers before I could catch it.

"*Be careful. I'm a patent attorney, and you may have*

committed the crime of copyright infringement. Are you aware of this?"

"I'm sorry, but there's no way you can protect yourself from my imagination. Besides, it's too late. I don't even know if I want to meet you. I may prefer to visit you in my dreams."

A pregnant pause went by before he replied, "Don't you need to meet someone and be with them first, before you can have something to fantasize about?"

"I don't. Your lips have already kissed me, and your hands have already caressed my entire body."

"I want to meet you, and I want that body picture."

"I don't know."

He had to get back to work, and I had to go put on a wig. *Ciao.*

* * *

On my walk through Chinatown, no one took much notice of me. Hmm. Maybe Paula would make a good spy?

I ruled out engaging in clandestine acts with this guy. First off, I didn't want anyone calling me fat. Second, he thought my name was Raya and that I looked like... Raya. The rejection potential was too high. And third, he probably assumed I was single.

Daydreaming was the only thing I was good for at the Open Center. Otto wasn't in, so I was left alone to run things. Or not run things, that is. So, to put an end to my dalliance, I sent Mr. Hot an email saying I only wanted to be with him in my imagination. (I also sent a carefully selected picture of myself in the hopes it would make him burn with unquenched desire.)

Then I thought about how he'd said he could tell just by our chatting that I was a writer, and that he *felt* my voice. That was so sweet.

An hour later, I logged back onto IM on Otto's computer. I'd just be online, sitting there, innocently. Soon after, Mr. Hot messaged to say that he got my picture and that I was a liar. First, because of my red hair, second because the picture looked too good to be true, and third it was another *face* pic.

"*You're probably fat and fucking around with me!*"

"*I AM NOT FAT!! THAT IS ME! GOODBYE!*"

"*Ok, ok, ok! I believe you! But why is your name 'Stacy,' and not 'Raya' on your email?*"

"*Well, I'm doing a social experiment. The hair colors, the names are all a part of it. That's all I'll say for now.*" I changed the subject by describing in detail what his hands and lips had done to me the night before.

"*I'm at work! Stop! You're killing me!*"

"*I know you're at work. I like to think of you there in that controlled corporate world, sitting in your office, reading my words and just wishing you could tear my clothes off. Are you wearing a suit?* "

"*I'm not giving you any more fodder for your imagination. No, you'll have to see for yourself, in the real world. Here's my phone number. Call me tonight at nine.*"

Shit. The real world; I didn't know how to do that.

Agent Thorn and I regrouped for dinner in the Meatpacking district at Son Cubano, a fun, crowded and loud place with great live Latin music. Some men smiled at us and we received nice treatment from everyone, except for one hostess who looked at me like I was a freak. Thorn also noted that two older fat men from the next table looked up when I went to bathroom. I'd say that amount of action qualified as under the radar.

Over tapas and mojitos, I filled Thorn in on my online antics.

"Nothing good can come of this!"

We bickered back and forth the entire night. It was a game of ours by now, and we laughed constantly. I loved outraging her, and she, in turn, loved telling me how outrageous I was. After a while, I conceded that she may have a valid point or two, but couldn't I just meet him for coffee?

She thought not.

It seemed destined to remain wishful thinking anyway. I couldn't figure out how I would get myself out of the wig situation.

"There's no way you're going to pull this off without him thinking you're wacko."

I glanced down at my phone and felt a nervous jab because it was a little after nine. Then I gave Thorn a pouting puppy look.

She tossed her napkin on the table. "Fine! Call him."

So I did.

We could barely hear each other above the commotion in the restaurant, but I loved his voice, and he was happy to hear mine. He was in a car on his way home to Hoboken.

"The lights on the hill are beautiful, and the view from the bridge is amazing. You'll see. You will love it."

Then we said goodbye.

"Stacy, there is NO WAY you are going to Hoboken with this man!" Agent Thorn glared at me.

* * *

Right as I was going to sleep, I received a text message from him wishing me sweet dreams and promising that I'd soon feel his strong hands on my skin. My imagination went into overdrive. I put on Peter Gabriel's *The Passion* soundtrack and drifted to sleep to the rhythm of tribal beats and visions of sin.

* * *

Date: Friday, October 28th
Fields of Research:
    Open Center 2:00 pm – 4:00 pm
    Posh uptown happy hour, 5:00pm – 7:00pm
    Penn Station Area 7:00 pm - late

* * *

My guilty conscious woke up right after I did.

I couldn't meet this guy. Even if I were romantically available, I didn't want to reveal my *real* self to him. God, he'd probably bring along a scale. No. I would keep the flirting strictly confined to my imagination. As soon as that was settled, I went online to just flirt.

First, I selected two of the most flattering full body pictures from the array of field shots taken during Raya's week. Then I added one I didn't like for a dash of realism. He responded to my email within minutes.

"I'm in love. When we meet, I'm going to kiss you, and if it's not what you've dreamed of, then I'll leave. I'll honor your decision."

My heart sank. *"Wait. I can't do this any longer. I have to make a confession. The experiment I'm doing, well, I change my hair color and stuff and wigs are involved. It is me in those photos, though."*

"I'm cool with that."

I don't think he really got it, but I didn't clarify. *"That's not all. I'm in a 'complicated' relationship situation."*

"I knew it was too good to be true. My friend warned me. I should've listened. He has good instincts about that sort of thing. Call me. Now. I'm not going to chat all day."

I called and he answered with, "Ok, now tell me."

The story of my dilemma between security and passion came tumbling out. He cross-examined me but otherwise remained quiet. Finally, he replied, "I just came out of a similar situation about a month ago. But maybe you could find both passion and security in one person. I took the risk. It was worth it for me." His calmness and apparent understanding shocked me.

"I'm so sorry. I really wanted to meet you."

"We can still meet. I'm not going to touch you, that wouldn't be right... but then again, if I don't touch you how will you be able to make your decision. Hmm. We'll see."

This took me by surprise, and I had to think for a second. "But what if you don't like me?"

"I already know I will. I'm sure of it."

"Come on, you can't be sure of anything. You don't really know me."

"I just know."

Oh boy, he's so mistaken was what I was thinking. A nervous flash came and told me he'd be disappointed in the real me, whoever that was, but I shooed the worry away. "Well, if it's just going to be having a drink together, then ok, why not. I'll probably be showing up as a brunette, can you handle that?"

* * *

As soon as Agent Thorn and I walked into the lobby of the St. Regis Hotel, our posh cocktail hour locale, I had an adverse reaction to the place. It looked like Liberace had had his way with the Queen of England's drawing room. Stuffygaudy.

Surely, this couldn't be the main entryway because dining tables were spread out in the large, open space. Was it a foyer with dining options or the actual restaurant? We spotted a hostess stationed at a podium, so Thorn went ahead and asked for a table for two for dinner.

The hostess looked us up and down several times and screwed her mouth around unfavorably before she announced, "Oh, all right." With a haughty sigh, she asked for Thorn's full name as well as mine.

"Oh, we're not staying at the hotel."

"It doesn't matter. I need them for my records. How do you spell your name?"

We told her, but she didn't write anything down. After another sigh, she crisply turned on her heel and motioned for us to follow with a disdainful head toss. Our table seating consisted of plush, living room furniture, and the table itself was low and of the coffee variety. Thorn sat on the divan, and I selected the armchair. The hostess stood there wincing. "May I take your coat?"

"No thanks, I'll keep it." I started to drape it across the back of my armchair, but she interrupted me.

"Excuse me, but we don't allow that here. You have to check your coat."

"Ah. I see." I answered politely and thrust it, none too gently, into her arms with a smile.

Thorn and I silently exchanged outraged faces and mouthed choice words as she walked away. We carried on our mute lip reading and hand motion dialogue for several minutes because the place was so deathly quiet, and we felt like shoplifters under surveillance. Our dining arrangement couldn't have been more uncomfortable, either. We were sitting on parlor furniture, and our table was so low we had to bend over to eat. I highly doubt she would've sat anyone but other undesirables here.

"Can you believe that? What a bitch!"

"I know! She had us spell our names and didn't even pick up her pen!"

"It killed her to seat us. I'm surprised she didn't start to bleed. And did you see her expression when she asked me for my coat? I think her lip actually curled! God. I'm mortified!

And outraged! My face feels like it's on fire. Is it bright red?"

"It's flaming."

"But do I look that scandalous? I mean, it has to be me because you could pass for a librarian in your beige outfit!"

"Well, your dress is short and racy for this place. Two young women coming into a place like this, and you dressed like that—We're hookers."

"No! Really? And I'm wearing the neutral, brown wig! What do you think they would've done if I were wearing the blonde, black, or red one?"

"Oh, they would have totally thrown us out."

Our initial feelings of humiliation and banishment passed, and we became amused and intrigued instead. After all, the joke was on them. I was in disguise, and we were here to observe how they treated me based on appearance. It made for excellent experiment fodder. Remembering that they were our research subjects helped me disassociate myself from the scorn, but I did experience moments of surrealism when I felt as if I'd done something very bad and was soon to be arrested.

A sole, impeccably groomed woman was dining near us. She ordered a bottle of wine and picked at her food, otherwise we were alone. The old money, conservative feel and the stuffy, gaudy decor didn't make for a lively atmosphere, either.

Thorn whispered, "God. I feel like I'm eating in a mortuary."

We started giggling. A moment later, an important looking man in a uniform swooped in.

"Is there anything else we can do for you ladies? May I suggest you order side dishes or vegetables?" He peered down at us like a disgruntled hawk. We knew his mission was not food related; he was serving us our "you're-not-welcome-here" notice.

"No. We're fine. Thanks." We smiled politely and waited

for him to leave. And then, just for that, we ate really slowly.

He had no reason to pick on us. We didn't order extra courses simply because we weren't that hungry, but even so, it wasn't as if we were being cheap. When in Rome, I spend like Caesar. My looks, not my finances, were to be my only questionable commodity.

"Should we go explore and see if we can find the hotel bar? I'm afraid of what will happen if we do, and I already feel like a lady of the night, but that's what we came here for. And I don't want the bullies to win."

"If you can handle it, then let's go."

We paid our bill, got our coats and went in search for the bar.

As we wandered deeper into our enemy's belly, my slip started to creep up. Sitting on the velvet armchair must've given me a bad case of static cling. The slip also acted as the lining for my crocheted dress, so every bit of creep revealed more of my bare body underneath. As soon as I tugged it down, it wriggled back up again. Why did this have to happen now?

When we entered the dark and crowded bar, the banter level immediately dropped to a whisper. It was similar to the hush that descends upon a crowd when someone calls for attention and is about to make a toast, but all we did was take a few silent steps inside. And then, like synchronized sparrows, we both did a U-turn and went back out. The communal disapproval literally repelled us and bounced us out of there like a force field. Besides, we felt certain someone would ask us to leave.

Everyone in there was kind of a blond, waspy individual in an 80's power suit. They weren't stylish, and they weren't old.

We retreated and were back in front of the hostess stand, now abandoned. Thorn went downstairs to use the restroom, and I stood alone, leaning on the wall, and checked my voice messages. I heard footsteps closing in behind me and turned to see three hotel workers, two uniformed men and the hostess, marching towards us in formation. One in the middle and two positioned to flank us from the sides. Thorn re-appeared, and I pushed her in the direction of the exit.

"Run!" We tumbled out of the revolving door and broke down into hysterical laughter.

"We just escaped within a hair's breadth from being kicked out!"

From there, we roamed around the area as we talked about what the hell I was going to do with the Internet guy.

"This rendezvous isn't really a big deal. I mean it's just the same if I met him in a bar and we started chatting. I've talked with lots of guys during the experiment. I'm only going to have a drink with him."

"Oh don't kid yourself; it's a date. It's premeditated. Face it. I'm really just concerned I'll get a call tomorrow morning and find out you're in Hoboken with some stranger. You *seem* like you're a psycho, but he could actually *be* one. He could kill you. Promise me you won't go to Hoboken!"

"I won't! But now you've made me nervous. Am I really a horrible person for doing this? It's not a date, *exactly*; all I want to do is talk with him. Maybe I should forget it. I'll just not show up!"

"Ok, ok. It's not *that* horrible. A good flirt is probably just what you need actually. That is, if you can keep yourself from going to bed with him. And above all, you can't confess! I think it's inevitable that you're going to have an affair if things keep going like this, but you're also incapable of keeping your mouth shut."

I was supposed to meet him at eleven at a bar in the area. It wasn't even eight yet, and I was jumping out of my skin. The first thing Thorn and I did in preparation for the occasion was buy a brush and a shellacking product to make my wig as non-intrusive as possible. Then we did a walk-by of the bar for a preview of the locale and to check out if this guy had any taste.

"Ok. If it's not an inspired choice, I won't go."

The neighborhood didn't hold much promise, but the bar was part of a boutique hotel and very nice.

"Hmm. Lovely. And attached to a hotel, how convenient." Thorn rolled her eyes and laughed.

"Quit it! It's just for a drink!" The preview of the dark and sexy bar sent me into new heights of anxiety, but I also couldn't wait.

We stopped at a Starbucks so I could change into my sexy green dress and primp. My wardrobe change meant the wig had to come off and then go back on, and I had to trade in my pantyhose for fishnet thigh-highs, all the while attempting to avoid stepping on anything gross. I was sweaty and annoyed, and someone had already started banging on the door.

A few minutes later, several voices were yelling, in Spanish, for me to hurry the fuck up. I told them to wait and then to go to hell, but it didn't help. And the zipper on the side of my dress was stuck. The pressure was getting to me, so I shoved everything into my bag and stormed past the barking family with my entire left side exposed. I did my best to look indignant and not crazy. When I turned the corner, Agent Thorn gasped.

"Oh my God! Why are you naked?"

I tried to hold the dress together but it wasn't working. We giggled like stupid schoolgirls and huddled in the middle of Starbucks as I yanked on the zipper.

"It's fucking stuck!"

"Ok, I know what to do, but first we have to get you out of here. We're causing a scene."

Our emergency response took place on the corner of a busy Times Square street. We tried to tuck ourselves into a corner, but my left breast kept falling out, apparently in plain sight, because throngs of tourists had stopped to gawk.

"Ok, ok. I know how to fix this. I've been in this situation before; I'll put some lip gloss on it." Thorn smeared it on the zipper, and I held my breast out of the way. She kept tugging and I kept sucking in but we weren't getting anywhere. We were traumatizing a flock of sightseers, and I was freezing.

"Make it work! I have to wear this dress!"

"I'm trying. Shut up!" The point of absurdity had long been passed when the zipper suddenly broke free and zoomed up. We scampered away and went along doubled over laughing for a few blocks.

All this commotion flitted me out. My nerve and confidence were leaving me fast. "I HAVE to go somewhere to check my hair. I didn't get a chance in there with those morons knocking the door down. God, I'm way too nervous. What if he doesn't like me?"

"I know what we can do; don't you think you need a drink or two to loosen up?"

"Absolutely!"

Thirty-four minutes to drink up some courage didn't seem like enough time, but it's all I had since I'd moved my rendezvous up by two hours. If I'd waited until eleven, I would literally have been sick. So Thorn and I ran into the first bar we found. It was an Irish pub and, in Thorn's charitable opinion, was *full of an awful crowd of total idiots.*

We made a beeline to the bar and ordered vodka tonics. I downed mine, ordered two more, threw back the second one, and headed for the bathroom. The stairs appeared to move around a little. As I clung to the handrail I thought, *Whoa. Don't get too drunk! I can't puke, and my face will get all red.*

Once in front of the mirror, I couldn't decide if I looked good or bad. I fussed around with my wig; then I checked out my ass. *Yep. I definitely have one, and why the fuck do I have panty lines? Should I take my underwear off? Am I scrumptiously curvy or just fat? He said he likes slim women. God. Do I look anything like my pictures? Oh Stop!*

I washed my hands, shook them dry, and gave myself a pep talk. After I finished my psychological bracing, I went back up and finished off Agent Thorn's vodka.

A wasted young woman and two chubby guys in ties, who we figured had to be her coworkers, sat at a little table near us. She spoke graphically and loudly about her lesbian experiments. "I couldn't stop kissing her titties!"

We decided she was in the city for a convention and would soon be back in a cubicle with these coworkers.

Her lewd chirpings randomly wove their way into my already altered state of consciousness. Suddenly she jumped off her stool, threw her arms up into a V for Victory stance, and screamed, "Freeeee-biiiiiiiiiird!" the moment the song began to play.

She almost startled me off my seat. That was my bizarro signal telling me it was time to go.

* * *

I walked into the mostly empty bar and felt horribly exposed as I searched for him. My breathing got shorter and shallower every time the steel knots tightened around my chest. By now there wasn't any room left for air to get in. A man was sitting in a dark corner, and he waved me over. Before I even had a chance to sit, he studied me and said flatly, "You look different." Followed by silence.

"It must be the hair." I answered with a smile as I took my seat next to him at the bar.

"No, it's something else. You look different." He looked away and started playing with the swizzle stick in his drink and then frowned into the bottom of his glass.

The blood drained from my body as the silence deepened, and I too stared at my drink. What happened to *I'll walk up to you without a word and kiss you?*

"I guess we have more to say online than in person," he announced with the fixed face of a stoic resigned to his fate.

"Well, I guess that's normal at first." I offered with a casual laugh.

"No, not necessarily."

I was buzzed but not drunk enough to ignore the rising panic in my gut. *Oh dear Jesus, I'm bombing here! How am I ever going to recover if my very first foray blows up in my face?* I excused myself and went to the bathroom.

My vision was a little blurred, but I looked in the mirror and didn't see anything wrong. I was alone and said aloud to myself, "I'm a pretty woman. I am. If he doesn't like me, whatever, that's ok. I am pretty, and I'm much, much more than that too."

In that moment, I really meant it and believed it, although I dreaded the thought of dealing with a rejected me in the morning. And besides, he didn't look the same in person either! If things didn't change fast, I was leaving.

The battle trumpet had sounded inside me though. No way was I going to go down without a fight. It wasn't a conscious decision. My mind flexed and leapt into hunting mode, and my entire body mobilized automatically. Then my will and mettle flipped down the faceplate and marched me back to my barstool. *YOU ARE GOING TO FALL FOR ME!*

Instantly, I became witty and funny. And sexual. My body held itself sensually, and I felt my cheekbones become more chiseled. My laughter softened and teased with flirtatious tones. I lowered my head slightly so I could look up at him with a tilted face and vixen eyes. My bosom chose to heave subtly, and I could feel my pheromones concocting more and more potent love brews. Cleverness and quick comebacks counter-pointed the physical. He couldn't stop laughing and warmed up a thousand degrees.

"You're so funny. Really, I can't believe it."

Neither could I! A oracle team of special seduction forces had stormed in and taken over. It had been years since these charm arms had seen active duty, but bless them, they didn't miss a beat! All I had to do was watch in awe.

"So, how was your 'research' tonight? And what exactly are you researching?"

"Oh Lord! My spy and I got kicked out of St. Regis because they thought we were ladies of the night!" Blurting this out as an explanation probably wasn't wise, but it worked as a gateway to lively conversation. I remained cryptic and revealed very few details about the actual experiment, but he was drawn into the intrigue. He moved in close and swiveled around on his stool so our bodies were facing each other. His eyes held my gaze intensely, and soon he began to touch my arm and brush my hand. Finally, I could breathe easier.

After enough time had passed, and I could tell he was hooked, I ventured, "so, how do you like this hair?" (I needed to be sure he knew it was a wig in case he started playing with it or kissed me.)

"What do you mean *this hair*?"

"I mean can you tell it's a wig?"

His eyes blinked fast and then got big and round. "What...? That's not a wig! You're playing with me. That's your real hair." Then he touched it and looked confused.

"That was part of my confession, I told you. Didn't I?" Turns out he missed that part and didn't understand the true meaning of *I'll be showing up as a brunette*. I had to show him that my scalp moved before he believed me.

He laughed and shook his head. "Damn. I had no idea. You're definitely *unique*..." He didn't pull away and didn't even inquire about my real hair. The small space between us disappeared, and my heart almost gave out.

"Would you mind if I had another drink?"

He seemed reluctant but then gave a small wave of permission with his hand. "If you wish." At first I thought he didn't want to have to pay for it, but after I ordered he told me why, "You really don't need another drink."

"What? I am perfectly in control here."

"No, no. You came in here drunk."

I reared back in outrage. "Drunk? Maybe tipsy, but not that bad!"

"You were feeling it. Trust me. I'm very skilled and practiced in observing the signs. The way your eyes slid to the side and rolled slightly when you looked at me and your languid limbs and dramatic body language. You're good at hiding it, but I can tell. It's usually a good thing, but I'm doing the opposite of what I usually do. I want to get you sober." He put his hands on my legs and continued, "I want to see what you're really like."

He wanted the *real* me. Upon hearing that, my soul hopped into his hands.

We went to that place where secrets are shared and startling revelations are made.

Both of us had been searching for the meaning of life since we were five.

"You went down the path of philosophy and mysticism, and I searched for God through science, but then I gave up. I wanted to believe so badly when I was a kid, but I think all we are is brain chemistry."

"No, no. We're so much more and there are so many different worlds and realities besides this one, trust me, I've lived in them."

"I love your boots."

"I love your smile."

"I think there's a fine line between madness and an open door to perception, although I think they are often intertwined. For almost two years, I was caught between the two, but there are real, yet seemingly impossible, discoveries to be made amidst the insanity. The trick is sorting it all out. The premonitions, clairvoyance, and telepathy that were part of a normal day for me back then were real, but I also believed I was the queen of Egypt and was bringing about the reincarnation of the Golden Race of Ra. I jumped out of a 'star gate' that just happened to be my shower; instead of landing in a different dimension I hit the bathroom floor and broke my jaw. God, I was so scared and trapped for so long."

"Oh no, Stacy, you can't tell me this now." He listened intently but then touched my face and touched a finger to my lips.

This startled me, and I realized I'd been saying too much without the least bit of filtering. I thought I'd freaked him out, and he'd simply heard enough, but he gently rubbed my cheek with his thumb and beheld me with the sweetest, most unguarded expression. Then he cradled his arms together and began rocking an imaginary baby to sleep. "You should only tell me these things when you're in my arms, so I can hold you."

His tenderness knocked the wind out of me, and I felt my eyes well up in gratitude, but I managed a smile and looked away. "Thank you, but it's ok. That was a long, long time ago. I've been fine for years. Really. It's just that I don't think you should give up. There's much more to life than you can see."

"You make me want to believe that." Then, with the fluidity that comes from infatuation and alcohol, we moved back into the moment.

Standing behind me, he massaged my shoulders and neck. His hands were strong and warm. "Your skin is like satin."

I leaned back into him as he caressed my face.

"Ah, I can tell it's a wig from this angle."

We collapsed into each other, laughing.

"Oh. Let me take your picture!" I pulled my camera from my purse and got ready to shoot.

"NO! No photos!"

"Why not? I want a picture!"

He grabbed my arm and we wrestled as I snapped away. I got a bunch of elbow, arm, and forehead shots. Then I got knocked off my bar stool, he caught me, and I gave up. We settled back down, and he caressed my legs, from the top of my thighs to my knees. I whispered things in his ear that I don't remember.

When we got up to leave, he went to the bathroom. I watched him walk away and then turned to stare at an abstract painting. The random, red splotches were starting to reveal their hidden meaning when he came up behind me and whispered in my ear.

"Are you ready, my Mona Lisa?" He grabbed my waist and whirled me around.

His lips were exquisitely formed, and his hands were holding me tight. I felt vaguely guilty.

We went outside and started walking. Midnight was a long time ago, but I didn't think our night was over. "You are 100% different." He stopped talking and looked very pensive, as if he were going over a legal briefing of our time together in his mind.

"Well, is that a good thing?"

"Well, mostly yes, but there are some parts that I'm not sure about. I think you are amazing and the most fascinating woman I think I've ever met, but some of the things you shared were a little weird for me. I haven't had a chance to really think about them."

"They're not *weird* because that qualification is determined in your own mind. They just are what they are."

He smiled a little wistfully and nodded to himself. "They are what they are."

I kept walking because I thought we were going somewhere else, but he grabbed me and turned me around. "It was so lovely to meet you." He pulled me in and kissed me, I felt no hesitation in his embrace, and it felt so good. I lingered there for a couple of moments but then broke away and left without a word. One more second and I would've woken up in Hoboken.

* * *

Date: Saturday, October 29th
Fields of Research:
   Aftermath of Last Night

* * *

"God, what have I done?" I felt like a baby sea lion that had somehow pulled through clubbing season. I raised my head up cautiously and noticed my cell phone was still clutched in my hand. After rolling over gently, I read the text message that was on the screen.

"*Sweet dreams.*"

That was from the night before, but I was sure by now he'd changed his identity and was in hiding. Did I really need to bring up the Golden Race of Ra? And Lord knows what other zany stuff went skipping out of my mouth, but these stories weren't funny underneath the surface. They scared me. I was afraid no man would ever want to be with me because I couldn't guarantee the stuff of these stories would stay in my past. And if it did come back to haunt me, I couldn't live through it alone. Who would sign on for that?

Well, Tim had, and he deserved to be thought of and treated as more than just a back-up safety net. I was being a selfish heel.

I'd felt such a spark and connection. More than I had with anyone in five years.

The excitement and possibility were palpable and

intoxicatingly real. This is what I wanted, but it was out of my reach.

Then Agent Thorn's voice invaded my mind and chided me. *It's only sex. Nothing more.*

No, she was wrong, but then I remembered something my *Hot or Not* guy mentioned early on,

"You know the hotel is connected to the bar, don't you?"

Quit crying and don't be so naive, I snapped at myself and crawled out of bed. But I was there, and I knew when something is genuine. He could've easily taken advantage of me, but instead he was sweet and open. Imaginary or real didn't really matter though, because it would never work. It was even written in our clothing. He wore cufflinks. I wore fishnets.

I'd be the one to let myself down gently though, not him. I sent him an email that afternoon so I could get it over with.

"*...Don't worry or feel bad if you don't know what to think about me. I may always be a human rollercoaster and unpredictable... As far as me expecting you to want to go out or whatever, I don't have any expectations. Besides, I have to figure out what I'm doing. I'm dying for passion and expanding horizons and living many flaming, shared moments in amazed expectation and even wonder, but the truth is I realize that my boyfriend has quite an enormous capacity for accepting me... but I'm so torn...*

"*Ok, no more messages, promise. I won't email or IM stalk you.*"

His response: "*Hi there Raya! It was a pleasure meeting you. I think you are awesome, but as you sensed, I was a bit worried you might be a stalker or something (which, of course, you are not)... truth is that given your shifting realities, there is no way you or I could be sure about anything... anyways I did feel a connection with you and really enjoyed your company. I am not sure, but our connection may have been only a momentary one, a porthole suddenly opening between two different worlds.*

"*P.S. regarding the hotel, while I did find you attractive, I was not suggesting anything at all...really.*

"*Enjoy your week.*

By greeting me as Raya, he told me I wasn't real to him anymore.

Chapter VI
Week Five: My Own Hair

It would be silly to write about the essence of who *I* am as I did for the other "girls." And it would be fairly impossible as well since, by now, it's obvious that I'm confused.

In preparation for my week, I went to a chi-chi salon in Soho for a cut and color.

This primping definitely wasn't cheating; after six weeks of being stuffed under a wig, my unkempt, tri-toned head would never occur in nature, or on purpose.

Being forced to sit in front of a mirror and stare at myself *au naturel* was so weird.

God, I looked bald. My nose was far too big for my face. Was my entire face too big?

Miraculously, my stylist swept in and saved the day. I left the salon with an auburny-brown shade not too far from my natural color and a smart, simple bob that fell halfway between my chin and shoulders. It didn't hurt to look at myself now! I was as ready as I'd ever be.

* * *

Date: Monday, October 31st
Fields of Research:
    Wall Street lunch, 12:00pm – 2:00pm
    West Village street time, 2:00pm – 5:00pm
    West Village happy hour, 5:00pm – approx 8:00pm

* * *

So, the moment I had tried so hard to forget about these last four weeks inevitably came to pass. I, Stacy, would have to go out into the world, without artifice and study what that looks and feels like. What if I found out I was fugly? What if I discovered all of my charms only work when I wear fake hair? What if I can't claim even one stare? I didn't like this, and it was Halloween. It seemed so unfair.

As I combed through my wet hair and parted it down the middle, I stopped and leaned into the mirror to take a closer look. *Wow, that's such a great part. It's so white and wide. Amazing! It really looks like a scalp. How'd they do that?* Then I remembered. *Because it's your own hair, dumbass!* Oh dear, I'd really lost all my bearings.

Once I finished getting ready, I popped in some blue contacts. No way was I giving these babies up. I still needed a little something to hide behind. I felt pretty pleased with what I saw in the full-length mirror. My hair wasn't dramatic or bounteous, but I thought it looked sleek and classy.

Now, stripped down to my bare self, instead of crumbling as I'd feared, I felt more solid, more anchored inside. I twirled around in celebration.

* * *

My cabbie flirted during our short trip to Wall Street. Then, as soon as I got out of the cab, a young man in a suit told me he loved my boots. Now this was the kind of start-off I needed!

Thorn and I made our way to our usual lunch area, Hanover Square, and chose a restaurant we went to during the blonde week. The same waitress served us as well. Of course, she didn't recognize me, but judging by her behavior, she definitely did not prefer blondes. Last time, she had sneered at me and blatantly ignored us, but now she smiled and treated Thorn and I to courteous and fast service.

During our Wall Street time, I filled Agent Thorn in on Friday night. "…We fell into our own space-time warp, you know? We spent an eternity together in a few hours. It was crazy; we've led parallel yet completely opposite lives… And you're wrong. It wasn't all about sex; it was special. He wanted to know the real me. He wanted to cradle me in his arms. I was his Mona Lisa…"

I recounted beautiful things he'd said and then told her about our emails afterwards. Thorn wasn't saying much, so I thought she was swept up along with me. "He felt our connection too, he couldn't deny it. 'A porthole opening between two different worlds', that's how he described it, and then ended the email with 'Enjoy your week'… OWWW OUCH!"

Thorn grasped my arm and jerked me backwards, none too gently, stopping us in our tracks. She stuck her hands in my face and kept pushing them towards me, as if she wanted to stuff my head into a box. She shook her own head with a look of impassioned disgust, her eyes fluttered uncontrollably, and she sputtered incoherent noises.

"NO WAY! STOP THIS RIGHT NOW! I cannot go along with this anymore! There is nothing, nothing, nothing you can read into 'Enjoy your week'! That means go away! 'Do not ever bother me again'!"

Her vehemence and volume shocked me.

I yelled back, "I KNOW! That was my point! That's what I was about to say! 'Leave me alone,' is exactly what it means! I'm not that stupid!"

"OK! With you, I just had to check."

We had a tense moment of after-shock and then felt mutually relieved. At least we agreed on this one, fundamental fact.

Here's Thorn's spy summary for the afternoon, although, I believe she was too outraged with me to execute her observation duties to the best of her abilities. I'd say she missed, at the minimum, seventeen looks.

Wall Street area 12:00pm:
15 looks while waiting for me (this is what you reported)
2 blue-collar 30s guys

At Waterstone Grill:
2 30s businessmen

Starbucks:
2 looks on way to bathroom

Back on street:
1 30s man

* * *

Date: Tuesday, November 1st
Fields of Research:
Soho Starbucks/street time, noon – 2:00 pm

* * *

After an hour in Starbucks, the goofy, giggling janitor had only briefly bothered me, and the plug-in guy, who sat across from me every week, had given me a slight, negative shake of the head. If I'd had more guts, I would have revealed my secret and asked for his input, but I just didn't see us being friendly. Nothing else to report. It felt great to be so light and cool headed. And I could scratch my head! Finding that I didn't care so deeply about my poor stare stat showing was a happy surprise, too. It bugged me but on an annoying mosquito level, nothing lethal, so far. A trying moment took place in front of the Starbuck's bathroom mirror. I swear half of me was missing.

Since covert observation wasn't really necessary, Thorn abandoned her outpost and joined my table. "What'd you end up doing for Halloween?"

"Tim wouldn't go to the parade with me. He hates crowds. And when I asked him to come over he gave me a lame excuse and then said, 'Why? I'd just disappoint you again.'"

"You better be careful. Your safety net sounds disgruntled."

"I know. And I should be doubly panicking. The first guy I've flirted with just confirmed my worst fears: My 'shifting realities' are too big of a liability for him. I feel so invigorated now, which makes me really not want to be around Tim. But if I fall without him around, I'll most likely go splat."

* * *

Date: Wednesday, November 2nd

Highlights from Soho barhopping, The Four Seasons, and therapy

* * *

Compared to all the other weeks, I was being a good sport and was a great deal less obsessed with myself. It was like the old poison paradox: too much can kill but a little can cure. I was sick of looking at myself, sick of seeking attention, sick of caring so much, and tired of all the emotional bouncing around that came along with this game. No magical transformation had occurred, but I was having more fun just being out and just being me.

Since I wasn't stirring up as much reportable action, here's a little highlight reel, low moments included, for the next few days.

* * *

The high point of Soho barhopping arrived when I noticed eight men couldn't take their eyes off me.

"Finally! Look, all those guys can't stop staring at me! Count 'em!"

"Um, I'm sorry to point this out, but there's a football game on the TV right above your head."

* * *

Power lunch Wednesday took place at the Four Seasons hotel restaurant. A bright, aqua contact popped out of my left eye as the waiter was taking our order. He jumped and let out a faint, surprised noise.

* * *

Leering, old men at Barnes & Noble helped us discover that my short hair allowed my cleavage to be on full display. I think my long locks must have acted as a shawl.

I kept tugging at the neckline of my dress. "Were my boobs always trying to escape like this?"

Here are my official findings:

Hair/Face Ratio, with my own hair= bigger face: bad.

Hair/Boobs Ratio, with my own hair= bigger and bolder boobs: good!

* * *

Official observation: This is the only week women didn't notice me.

* * *

Thorn took some field snapshots one afternoon, and I felt gravely dismayed.

When I told her I was going to delete them, she grabbed the camera away. "But my hair's flat, and I look jowly and fat-faced!" I protested.

"You've got to have some less flattering pictures, too. You can't just edit them out because you want to always look pretty. What's the point of taking pictures to document how you look then?"

"Fine, whatever."

It pained me to keep them, though I was edging closer to accepting myself. It was as though I had been growing a real-me seed inside a wig-covered greenhouse.

* * *

1 30s man in restaurant (attractive)
1 30s cell phone guy
1 40s man in lobby as we (discreetly!) took pictures

And then for the twenty minutes or so of walking in Midtown:
Street:
1 look older man
1 30s guy
1 20s guy
1 30s man looked
During all that talking, these people were watching: Barnes & Noble Upper West Side:
2 old guys (the old guys at B&N love you!)
1 young man
2 looks on your way to get books
1 old man "sort of tried to rub against me" (per you)

* * *

My therapist ticked me off regularly, but at the moment, I loved her.

"Don't worry. It was harmless. You were determined to have a magical experience, so you went out and found one. That's all. It doesn't really matter who it was, but thank God you reigned in your lust and didn't create some sex trauma."

As soon as she said "harmless," I felt blessedly absolved from my drink-date sin.

"Couldn't you just get by with little flirtations like this until we're more sure you are ready? It's not a healthy situation for either of you, but we don't want another botched break-up job."

I felt bad about all of this premeditation. I didn't want to be evil.

* * *

Date: Thursday, November 3rd
Fields of Research:
    Open Center 2:00pm – 6:00 pm

* * *

"You look gorgeous today!" My cab driver was a chatty and feisty old man.

"Who, me?"

"Yes you. Who else is in the cab?"

"Oh, ha. I thought you were talking about the weather."

"You're not a native, are you?"

"No, I'm from Illinois, but I've lived here for a couple of years."

"Oh, that's good, but you have to be here for ten years before you're considered a native. Have you found someone?"

"Found someone? As in a guy?"

"Yeah, have you found yourself a man yet?"

"… Um… yes."

He grinned and whistled. "Well, you're lucky! Most girls I talk to are frustrated. They tell me it's terrible out there. So hard to get a good man! They say the West Village is gay, East Village the guys are all drugged out and want someone to take care of them; they want a mommy not a girlfriend. Then on the Upper East Side, they have to fight with two other women for an interesting man." He was a total character and had been gathering his data over the last twenty years. "Well, you should keep your guy. He's doing something good for you. You look good."

"Thanks. And don't worry, I will." His concerned face eased into a relieved smile.

I lied to avoid hearing him tell me I was doomed.

"Now let me tell you how I met my wife here, right here in Manhattan, over thirty five years ago. Things weren't the same, you know …"

* * *

"Oh my God, I didn't recognize you!" The receptionist howled when I arrived at the Open Center. "Y'all come here and look!" A bunch of people gathered around, touched my hair, and patted my head as if they were feeling up a pregnant belly. "You know I think a part of you has gone into that hair. It's changed you a little bit; your energy is different."

"Yeah, I think I'm more cheeky."

"Yeah, you are." She laughed and did a little diva dance for me. "Go girl, go girl!"

"I don't know what your deal is, and you can just stop your whining." Otto rolled his eyes when he saw me. "It's fabulous hair. You look like Toni Collette."

The Assistant Director, who had prayed for my cancer recovery, popped into the Wellness office. "So, is this your real hair?"

I nodded.

"Well, it looks good. So, what's all of this for?"

"It's all been an experiment…"

"People knew it was a wig though, right?"

My cheeks turned scarlet. "No. Actually no. Maybe a few women, but I think the guys were clueless."

"Well, the straight guys you mean. It's hard to pull the wig over the eyes of a gay man."

I could handle it if a gay man could tell. I didn't know or care if that comment meant he was actually gay, but I hoped so for my ego's sake.

If people knew I was wearing a wig, who cared, I told myself. Why not think of it as a fashion accessory, kind of like a rhinestone belt, or akin to a special filter used in Photoshop®. I liked that. I had photoshopped myself. What of it?

A young guy, who I'd never talked to before, flashed me a big grin when I passed him in the hallway.

"Wow, your hair always looks so different every time I see you and always so good."

I laughed loudly at him. "Well, this is my real hair, so I'm glad you like it."

"What do you mean your real hair?" Turns out, he was straight and clueless.

"So, which one do you like the best?" I asked, shyly.

"This one." He laughed.

"Really?! Well, that's cool since it's mine, but I'm surprised. Don't guys have a thing for lots of long hair?"

"Nah. You just need enough to grab onto." He said with a cheeky grin.

* * *

Agent Thorn showed up Thursday night with blonde hair. Not fair! She wasn't supposed to go off and get highlights! As we walked from Soho to the Meatpacking District, I protested, silently of course. *It practically lights up the night around her. Those guys looked at her! For crying out loud, it's so blonde, and there's so much of it!*

The bartender at our first stop wasn't nice, and the ambience matched his hard-edged aloofness. It felt like a red-hot poker was branding me over and over with a reject mark. I wanted to run or at least slip out of myself and hide, but the only place I had left was behind my drink.

"God. I need more make-up, something, just give me a little more cover-up. You know, kind of like training wheels or Methadone."

Walk to Meatpacking District
1 very tall man
1 homeless man with cart
1 look from man with weird fur hat
1 biker guy kind of sneered

Gaslight
(We briefly went in, were horrified at meat market/frat party atmosphere and left)
2 looks from meathead 20s guys

Windsor (upstairs at Gansevoort Hotel)
Again we just walked in, strolled around a bit, and headed out. We were being finicky. Appalling crowd of date-rapist looking finance guys, and hair ponies.
1 look there.

Street
1 30s Eurotrash guy

* * *

Date: Friday, November 4th
Fields of Research
    Posh uptown happy hour, 5:00pm – 7:00pm

* * *

My big stare-stat windfall—forty-one!—came during a quick café stop on Friday night. Agent Thorn claimed these numbers were misleading since we were the only dummies who sat outside drinking in the cold, and that alone caused curiosity.

"You can't prove that! And look, two more people are sitting outside now. Ha! Now maybe I won't come in last!"

Outdoor Restaurant Café
26 looks from men
6 from women
1 smile from old guy

Street
3 men
2 women

Tao Restaurant Bar
Wink from bartender
2 looks from 40s men
3 other assorted looks
1 look on way out
1 older woman stared
    1 repulsive lounge lizard checked us (and every other female)
out.

* * *

Thorn and I couldn't believe the experiment was almost over. Thinking about it made me sad. Next week we only had a handful of make-up days to do and then that was it. We reminisced fondly over our last call beers.

"I think this has totally prepared us for Internet dating," said Thorn. "We've been with each other almost every day and night for five weeks without running out of things to talk about. Really, we're expert banterers now."

"A lot of our chatting wasn't exactly date material though. We can't talk about hair, guys, or spying, but then again, we won't be going on 200-hour dates. Or you won't that is; why am I even including myself! What if I go back to crosswords in bed?" I already missed everything and had no idea what I'd do after this.

"I have a feeling you won't."

* * *

Date: Saturday, November 5th
Fields of Research:

Lower East Side late night bar scene, 10:00pm – early am

* * *

Steve's emergency services were enlisted for Saturday night. Thorn called in sick.

He had never seen me with real hair, and we hadn't seen each other since our kissing incident. As I got ready, I grew leery of his reaction.

He came to my place, and I opened the door with a grand flourish and presented myself to him. He gave me a funny look.

"Well?" I asked, nervously.

He squinted at me. "Ok, you're still hot. You look great, definitely hot, but not white hot."

Sweet, thanks for the downgrade. Then he proceeded to act bored and out of it. His complete 180-degree behavior turn did wonders for my confidence. I started to feel shaky.

It soon became evident that Steve was stoned out of his gourd. He was worthless, but I dragged him out anyway and fed him, in the hope he'd come around. I wanted to blame his lack of enthusiasm all on the pot, but after his bemused picture taking in the cab, it got too personal. He snapped away and gave me a running commentary.

"Oh, that's a bad one. That's definitely not good—delete. Wow, now *that's* a delete!"

Over dinner, I tried to subtly request that he quit hurting my feelings. "Hey, I need you to help keep my confidence pepped up, especially on *my* night."

He nodded his head but kept shoveling in his tuna tartar instead of answering.

I tried to stop myself, but I whined. "You used to compliment me and tell me I was white hot all the time and kept me revved and egged me on."

Steve put his fork down and rested his hand atop mine. "Well, honey, you still are, but you can't tell me to do that because then it wouldn't be real. It'd be like repeating lines, you know, it has to be spontaneous."

Well, fuck you and you can pay for your own dinner. I took my hand back, smiled and bit off my tongue. I wanted to go home.

I flirted with a few guys, and enough interest was stirred up to record, but without Steve's boisterous cacophony of praises accompanying me, I felt like a desperate ho in my outfit. I convinced myself I had a *good enough* time.

Chapter VII
Week Six: Make-Up Days Assorted
Hair Colors

Date: Thursday, November 10th
Fields of Research:
    Miscellaneous Cafes
    Internet Dating and Psychiatry

* * *

Thorn and I loitered in a café, making up for some missed research time. We hadn't seen each other for a couple of days, so I filled her in on my latest Internet activities which included meeting a Special Forces soldier.

"You know the Special Forces soldier I told you about from *Hot or Not*, well he is so beautiful. His body, his eyes, his words, everything. And he's got a web cam, so I get to watch him while we chat online and talk on the phone. Then last night we went hunting. You know, I was the prey that no hunter could ever catch, but he promised he'd be the one to kill me with his masterful arrow, plunged into my flesh without mercy."

"Oh, please! Gross! Stop!"

"I'd die to go meet him. Maybe I could just catch a plane…"

Agent Thorn slammed her coffee cup on the table. "You're *not* going to North Carolina to meet some guy who's said he wants to kill you!"

"Oh come on, it was a metaphor. Besides, I was the one who started it."

"I have no doubt you started it, but that's what he does, he's a trained killer. How do you know he's not serious?"

"Oh, he's still in training, and he's not that way."

"Oh, a killer *in training*. Sure, go on down there."

"Well, I'm going to get a web cam then."

"Don't. You will either write the book or get a camera. One or the other, but if you do one, the other isn't going to happen."

We wrapped up our loitering and took a taxi back to my place. Halfway there, the cab driver piped up.

"Hey, do you ladies need any electronics? If you do, well, I know of this great store in Chinatown, right near here. They've got everything, best prices around."

"Well, actually, yes, I do! But do they have web cams?" I elbowed Thorn in the side.

"I'm sure they do. Got everything. In fact, I need to go there myself; I'll just drop you guys off."

I squealed. "This is a total sign! It's meant to be!"

Thorn rolled her eyes.

"Ok, great, we'll go!"

"I'll have you know that just because I'm with you, this does *not* mean I condone this. And it's *not* a sign!"

We stood where the cabbie left us, right in front of the store doors.

"Please! I just said ten minutes ago that I wanted a camera then our cab driver intervened, like the hand of God, and brought us here! Even you can't deny that's weird. We're here, we have to go in and look." I giggled maniacally.

Thorn was had! How could she not see this was at least a nudge of Fate?

I got the camera.

Soon I was modeling lingerie and doing stripteases for the soldier. He got to know and love all of the "girls" since I showed up in a different wig every night. And my worries that I'd look like a cow were erased the moment he saw my body. My eyes never left his as I slowly slipped off one camisole strap and then the other. He leaned in and a look of longing, awe, and I swear, pained reverence transformed his handsome face.

"You're a breathing statue. Beautiful, so beautiful... And you look so natural and comfortable with yourself."

I sat there bathing in bliss.

Meanwhile, my real life boyfriend and I barely talked, but the elephant never left the room.

* * *

During the experiment, I had made and achieved a private goal: no psychiatric interference. I had canceled an appointment with my psychiatrist, telling him I wouldn't have time for one until my research was over. Not untrue! Well, now I guess I had time.

"I'm fine, I'm fine. Don't worry," I said when he called. "How about next week?"

"Great, but I think you may be a lot more than fine. That's what I'm worried about." He wanted my butt in his office now.

* * *

I sat down, rested my hands on my lap and tried to appear nice, calm and even. "What?! I'm fine!"

"Hey, I didn't say anything."

"You don't have to, you're giving me that look! I may be

a little more up now, sure, but I'm totally in control. Really."

"Ok, but you are kind of high. It's written all over you. And you know you're most likely going to keep ramping up. That's the problem. Maybe we should re-think some meds, just to slow this upswing down a bit."

"No! I'm far from manic. And I just got over five months of depression hell. I know I can't spin out, but I finally feel good, inspired."

"Well, how revved up is your mind?"

"My thoughts have sped up a little, and I'm connecting more dots lately, but nothing dramatic."

"Have you been seeing 'signs'?"

"No... Well, ok. A few, but it's not like I really believe them," I said.

"And your libido? It's skyrocketed. You said you're ready to explode."

"Oh come on, that's natural! I'm sex starved! Anyone else in my position would be dying for it, too."

I left his office with a compromise. We would just keep an eye on things, but I had to come back in a week.

* * *

Date: Sunday, November 13th
Fields of Research:
  Cyberdates with a Soldier

* * *

The Soldier and I listened to music together during our "dates." A track from Peter Gabriel's *Passion* album was our song for the night.

"You're right Stacy, it's amazing. And it has that organic, hypnotic rocking motion that's perfect for sex. Now, just imagine how it would feel to be entwined, skin on skin, with the bass and drums vibrating through our bodies."

We promised to play it as we went to sleep and make love with each other in our dreams.

Here's a random journal entry of mine around this time:

My God, how is it that I can live without this! I want to be devoured; I want to be captured and afraid with my face on fire, nervous and taut with want ... abandoned and absorbed in the moment. He will lead me there.

Chapter VIII
Experiment Aftermath: The Boys

Date: Wednesday, Nov. 16th
Fields of Research:
 Mischa

* * *

With the experiment now officially over, the threat of falling back into my previously stunted life panicked me. I needed to find a way, besides cyberspace, to keep up my social momentum. I started by going on a "platonic" date with a Russian diamond dealer I met on *Hot or Not*. He said he was looking for friends with whom he could enjoy the city's cultural riches and mentioned that he usually had an extra ticket to the hottest shows. His picture didn't reveal much since he sported big, black sunglasses, so all I could gather was that he had dark, shoulder-length hair, pale skin, and liked baby blue sports jackets. I suspected he had to bribe women to hang out with him, but I wasn't above a free show. I agreed to accompany him to a dance performance.

He piled on the flattery when he wrote me. The subject line of his first email was, "*Of all those arts in which the wise excel...Nature's chief masterpiece is writing well....*" Then he continued with praise for the moving words of my profile.

I decided to wear my red wig and blue contacts for the

occasion. I figured he'd get over it if he usually preferred blondes. We met at a pastry shop early that evening, and he seemed delighted with what he saw. He greeted me with a grand flourish of kisses and immediately ordered us one of every cake on display.

When I protested and pointed out that we could never eat a dozen cakes, he replied, "They exist for you to taste, my dear. How could I allow for you to know just one? I could never forgive myself if your lips were wanting for anything."

Once seated, I had a chance to really look at Mischa and decided he was handsome in a disconcerting way. He was tall, but managed to be both gangly and doughy. He had lots of long dark hair, which was a plus. His manner was exceedingly flamboyant, even spasmodic. Everything was elevated to a high level of grandeur, but he didn't quite pull off the show. He reminded me of a little boy all dressed up in a tux with tails. Mischa's Russianness and accent intrigued me, plus, he really loved my "bounteous" red hair. As we bit into cake after cake, Mischa gazed upon me with his big, puppy-brown eyes in reverence.

At the café, I mentioned a few things about my experiment but wouldn't tell him exactly what it was.

He didn't seem surprised or confused. "You haven't merged with these personalities have you? Have you lost yourself?"

"No, I'm perfectly aware who I am, and I'm not five different people."

He smiled and reached for my hand.

He insisted on putting his arm around me as we walked to the theater and kept nuzzling up and planting kisses on my cheek.

I told him to stop.

He explained it was a Russian cultural thing and that he meant nothing by it. "You people here in the West do not understand intimacy. I do this with all my friends; we think nothing of it as it is natural and beautiful."

What a line of bullshit. I let him get away with it, however, because I liked being fawned over, although he started to creep me out.

Once we were seated in the theater—and all through the dance performance—he continued plastering the side of my face with kisses and started trying to aim for my mouth. He insisted on cuddling as he nuzzled, pawed, and smooched my hair/wig.

I wriggled away and reminded him that we weren't on a date.

He whispered into my ear, "I would trade a thousand orgasms for the chance to look into your eyes and touch your hair, my dear."

I guffawed loudly at this and informed him unceremoniously that I was wearing a wig. That didn't faze him. So, I tried to pretend he wasn't there. We did have amazing seats, and I did love the performance.

Afterwards, we walked around for at least an hour as he told me about his life and his love for me. He proclaimed that from the very moment he saw me he knew we were members of the same tribe.

"And that tribe would be?" I prompted.

"The crazy ones, the mad geniuses, the Romeos and the Juliets; the ones who travel through the valley of death to get to the other side and drag the devil out into the light. Us, we, you and I, my dear, and our beloved brothers and sisters. We are rare indeed because we are alive, and now for you and I to have come together and joined forces on this night... do you know what this means to me?"

He stopped and put his hand into his pants pocket and then pulled something out. He opened his fist, and in his palm laid four pills of different shapes and colors. "It means you will understand. Women who aren't touched by fire can never comprehend the unending well of my pain or the infinite stratospheres of my joy." He put the pills back in his pocket and began describing some of the events that led to his discovery that he was bipolar.

"You know, I had a revelation the last time I came to the point of killing myself." He went on. "I sat on the edge of my bed at three in the morning, with the darkness around me illuminated by two dozen flickering white candles and the red shot glass full of arsenic clutched in my hand, and that's when I decided. I screamed, I CHOOSE LIFE! FUCK IT! I CHOOSE LIFE! And I threw the glass against the wall and have not wasted a moment since. That was a year ago…."

Perhaps he was right about me because none of this struck me as particularly odd or alarming. In fact, I was enjoying being a part of this tribe for the evening and listened without protest.

After a good deal of this kind of talk, the subject switched to diamonds. He'd told me during our cake-eating spree that he worked in the diamond district as a diamond dealer.

"How can you feel good about selling diamonds when people are murdered, maimed, and exploited in so many of the places where they are mined? Isn't it akin to dealing in blood?"

"Well, my dear, I do not pretend to be a saint, and I do not find the glory of God in diamonds. But in this world everything is touched by the dust of death, and it is all I know since I was a child. It is what I do."

"Ok, fair enough, so tell me what's it like? How does it work? What's the diamond district all about?"

What he told me was fascinating. My favorite part was learning about the diamond dealer's vest. I'd noticed the gray satin vest underneath his cobalt blue jacket earlier, but it had confused me. It reminded me of a gunslinger's garment but something about the cut didn't look right. Well, it angled back under the arms for a reason. He opened up his jacket, tugged on the vest and looked at me. "What do you think we do with the diamonds? We carry them on us.

How else are we going to sell them? Thieves would rip a bag, a briefcase, or my pockets right off of me, but like this, with the diamonds inside this vest pocket and right under my arms they'd have to rip me in half to get to them."

At the end of our long walk, we stopped at another café. That's when I found out he still lived with his parents somewhere out in Brooklyn.

"What? Why do you still live with your parents all the way out there?"

"It's fine… I never sleep … I never go home. It saves me money, so now I can buy whatever I want. Why do I need a place of my own when I never sleep? I either walk around the city all night, or I go to a girl's house at three in the morning and then go to work. I never sleep." He waved his hand in the air as if he were shooing a gnat away. "Those girls are not like you; they mean nothing to me."

By now, his insistent hugging and kissing had kicked in again, and I suddenly wanted out of the tribe. Over our final cappuccino, he looked into my eyes and talked about finding The One. He whispered, "I pray it's you. I have waited so long."

"Hmmm… well, thanks, it was great. It's late… bye."

By the time I'd gotten home, he'd already called twice, left two messages, and texted me three times. The following day, the emails started to flood in. I went out with him again a couple of days later, mainly because he promised to wine and dine me to the tune of live jazz at Birdland and take me to see Balkan music performed by Bato de Yugo at some mysterious place in Alphabet City. Wild gypsy music is another one of my weak points.

I arrived at Birdland, but Mischa was nowhere to be seen. The hostess inquired if she could help me, and I replied, "I'm here to meet Michael Katsabatatavaka," which was the best I could do with pronunciation, but it sounded nothing like his last name.

She brightened and repeated his name the way it was supposed to sound. "You must be Stacy. Michael told me you were a very special guest of his and that he will be arriving shortly. We are so happy to have you here with us this evening. Please follow me. We have a V.I.P. table right in front of the stage reserved for you. He has also requested that you enjoy a glass of champagne while you wait. Is that to your liking?"

"Sure."

After the jazz show, Mischa went up, smothered the lovely, young singer with kisses and then introduced us. "The moment I heard her sing five years ago, I knew she would be recognized as the queen songbird that she is, and I was right." He enthusiastically recounted her key performances.

He acted so overly grandiose that I felt sorry for him. His attempts at playing the part of extravagant royalty were awkward; I could tell people humored him because of his money and were quick to disengage. As we mingled around the bar, it became apparent that he was also clumsy and bumped into people all over the place. Again, he reminded me of a lonely little kid playing the part of a Czar playboy. But my sympathy would soon evaporate.

As soon as the door of our minivan cab slid closed, he pulled my face towards his with his right hand and kissed me while his left hand roamed all over my legs. I shoved him off and slapped at him in an attempt to fend him off as we sped downtown. I yelled for him to stop, but he was undaunted. He smiled, grabbed, and kissed as he recited Russian poetry and whispered, "Stolen kisses are one of the greatest pleasures in life my dear. I will win your heart."

I wasn't outraged, just grossed out, but I kept thinking, *Jesus, this gypsy music had better be good.*

Thankfully, I was rewarded for my suffering. Bato and his electric gypsy band hit me like a lightning bolt and filled the small bar with chaotic and magic music. Bato's craggy, hard-edged but incredibly rich voice, combined with the insistence of the violin's exquisite, pleading agony sent me into throes of ecstasy. I danced and twirled and kept locking eyes with Bato. I felt like a true gypsy in my short bohemian skirt that was perfect for twirling. I was alive and on fire with *Kali's* long red hair flying and hanging down my back, all sweaty and tangled.

But then there was Mischa. He kept trying to teach me the traditional Georgian dance, the one where your arms are raised to the sky and you twist your hands about up there while you circle around and do cross over moves and turns with your lower half. Bah, I just wanted to move with the music and twirl. I'd do his damn dance with him for a while and then go back to my own thing, but he wouldn't stop coming up behind me and pressing and grinding his pelvis against my ass. Ugh, I could feel his little dick pricking me. That did it. I decided that even if he invited me to dinner with *Bono,* it wouldn't be worth going out with him again.

Later, he insisted on sharing a taxi with me. I said no fifty times, but he jumped in anyway. He kept kissing my hair—didn't he get it that it wasn't mine? My warning bells were shrieking, so I had the cab driver drop me off a couple blocks away from my place. I literally had to push him back into the cab to keep him from following me.

* * *

Fields of Research:
    Tim
    Stephen
    Steve

* * *

Tim was angry with me. I told him I was meeting someone for a drink and then going to a party at Steve's that night. He was upset that I never invited him to meet my new friends.

"Well, you never want to go out when I invite you anyway. You always have to work."

"Well, what if I do want to go to the party?"

I told him he could come if he wanted and gave him the address of the party.

"I'll call and probably meet you there later."

Just thinking about having to behave and hang around him made me groan. I imagined being at the party as a couple, and it really pissed me off. He had called me on it. It wasn't about him wanting to go, and we both knew it. He was making a point, albeit a belated one.

I had an early evening rendezvous with another guy from *Hot or Not*, before the party. This dude's profile said he only wanted to make friends if "*...you want to get down with my girlfriend, too.*"

Well, turns out, he wasn't joking, and he opened my eyes to the existence of polyamorous relationships. Stephen and his girlfriend wanted to find that perfect someone to have a serious relationship with them both— a threesome. I was very intrigued, even though it wasn't what I wanted. Still, I liked him, and I craved the thrill of pushing my boundaries.

I sent Stephen a couple of my songs.

He emailed me, "*We both fell in love with them. I hope you don't mind that I shared your music with Allison, but listening to them was such a powerful experience for me that I had to. She is part of my soul, so she had to hear them, and she could feel your liquid eroticism pulsing through your voice.*" He offered to give me his girlfriend's email, so I could get to know her.

That kind of blew my mind. Nothing wrong with it, but I couldn't imagine flirting with a girl and being considered a prospective lover for both of them. I didn't take him up on that but did agree to meet him alone for a drink.

I've always been open-minded, but the experiment had stretched my thinking even more.

My ideas of sexuality had expanded; my exploration of myself through the different 'girls' had yielded insights and the desire to discover more. Now I had drawers full of sex outfits, and my libido was on fire. The pre-wigged me wouldn't have considered talking with a polyamorous man on the prowl for a third wheel.

Surprisingly, Agent Thorn thought that a poly relationship might work for me—but definitely one with two men, not another woman. In a perfect world, one would be the calm, stable, caring lover and the other the wild, crazy, artist monster. Of course, we both foresaw it ending in jealousies and tears, but it could be good for a while.

* * *

Sitting next to Stephen made me feel like a chunky Amazon. I wore a new brown curly lion's hair wig, which added to my girth, and my ankles probably weighed more than he did. He was good-looking in an extremely svelte and precise way. He had very short strawberry blonde hair, fine bone structure, angles everywhere, and wore square-rimmed glasses. One moment I saw him as masculine, but the next second he seemed extremely feminine. He told me a story about an actor he and his girlfriend had dated over the past summer:

"It was intense and a lot of things worked, but the guy was young and somewhat emotionally immature. I just couldn't mesh with that."

Who knows what he thought of me. I was wearing velvet and sparkly costume jewelry topped off by a huge head of fake hair. Horrible visions of me looking preposterous with gold thread unraveling from my scalp came to my mind, but

I couldn't read him. When we went outside for a bit so we could escape the music and talk freely, I blabbed on and on about the experiment. He seemed intrigued, but was just too damn quiet. I had all that empty air space to fill, and I ended up being a giggly motor mouth.

When Stephen did get chatty, he talked about his girlfriend, and this dreamy look washed over him. His eyes became gauzy, and he looked into space wistfully. "There's no one like her; no one as beautiful. We are one."

I asked him how they could do this, and why would they want to since they were so in love and soul matched.

"That's exactly why we can and why we want to."

I was confused. It was all cool with me, but I was only sightseeing. In all, it was a pleasant, short meeting. It never went any further.

I headed out to a birthday party at Steve's place in Brooklyn. My curly look was new, and I'd already found the reactions to my bounteous head to be radically different from the other wigs. Women loved it, and from what I'd observed, they considered me to be as threatening as a cute kitten.

The day before, at a Barnes & Noble checkout counter, I noticed that the young woman ringing up my purchases was scrutinizing my hair. It made me painfully paranoid, but when I leaned over to sign the credit card slip, she gushed, "I just have to tell you that I adore your hair. You have so much. You are so lucky."

Men, on the other hand, didn't seem to pick it up on their radar, and if they did it was more of a slow burn. But I liked it, and I arrived at the party feeling on.

Steve's apartment was a huge, open loft space and full of interesting characters that hailed from strange and exotic places, like Wisconsin and Montenegro. I knew some people there through both Steve and Nikoleta, and I mingled, chatted, and fluttered from group to group. This was a big change from the old, socially paralyzed me. The social graces/dating boot camp Agent Thorn and I had put ourselves through had worked wonders for my feeling at ease with people, and I got to hide any lingering insecurities behind my big wig, too.

It also helped that Steve made me feel at home by rushing to my side with hugs and kisses and his trademark exclamations of, "You're off the hook," and, "White hot."

The only thing that put a damper on my fun was the thought of Tim showing up, but that weight was lifted when he called to say he wouldn't make it after all.

I overheard an attractive man remark to his friend, in French,

"It is a true shame we are forced to drink beer. How could one think of having a party without wine?"

Once he took a swig of the dreadful brew, I said, in French, "Yes, it's a shame you didn't bring wine and treat us all to a civilized beverage."

"Ah, tres bien, so you understand French, eh?"

I'd had more than a couple of beers by this time, so everything that came out of my mouth traveled straight from the lower regions of my brain sans filter. Perhaps I made a bad translation error, but soon we were talking about cannibalism. I went on about the true story of an American missionary working in the Peruvian Amazon that left Jesus to join one of the tribes living deep in the jungle. Everything was swell for a while. The missionary and the tribesmen all hunted, shared meals, slept, and fucked together peacefully until the cannibalism part reared its ugly head. One night they dragged him along unawares into a raid on another village where they killed everyone and then carried home the best male parts for the flesh eating ritual called the Jaguar Ceremony.

"Imagine: all of these men, on a full moon night, joined together in a circle in the heart of the Amazon, illuminated by flames as they devoured their quarry. Then, with other men's blood dripping over their naked bodies, they closed the circle by fucking each other like jungle beasts and roaring into the night like Jaguars."

I paused and reflected for a moment and concluded, "Obviously there is deep primal eroticism, enormous feelings of power and I'd imagine intense bonding that goes on in a communal-killing, flesh-consuming, and fucking experience, and you know *when in Rome...* but I think he really crossed the line on that one. Then again, who am I to judge?"

The French man looked at me with what I can only describe as a famished look and replied, "I'm an epicurean."

Maybe I'd become the jungle beast and was taking this hunt for a monster of a man a little too literally.

We parted ways with him saying he wanted to see me again so he could immerse me in French culture.

* * *

When I got home, I had an email waiting for me from Agent Thorn: "*I hope you realize, my friend, that you are now dating.*"

Damn her!

Happily, the soldier was waiting online for me, too. I told him about my search for U2 concert tickets. We had both loved their music since we were twelve.

"I haven't found anything great for NYC, but I did find amazing seats on eBay for the Boston concert in early December. For a giddy second, I thought to myself, 'maybe he could come.'"

"Who's 'he'?"

"You, of course."

"I'm ninety-percent there already."

"What? Really?!"

"Buy them, and I'll do everything humanly possible to be there. I'll put in for leave, get a plane ticket, and make it work. I will."

I squeezed my eyes tight to shut out any reason and pressed the "Buy-it-Now" button.

* * *

Date: Sunday, November 20th
Fields of Research:
    Tim, The Soldier, and Advisors

* * *

I awoke and remembered that my first step towards hell had been taken. With the sin-stepping now in motion and the concert only two weeks away, I had to just do it.

I headed out to Soho to spend the afternoon writing in a café. As I passed the big Confucius statue near my apartment, I called Tim.

"What's up?"

"We have to talk." I blurted it all out, "Things just aren't working. We're on two different planets. We both know it. I think we're meant to be friends."

Nothing on the other end. My stomach dropped.

"Well, I'm glad you're bringing this up. I've been thinking about this for a while also, and I think you might be right."

I started crying.

He assured me he'd always be in my life, that we had an inseparable bond and I wasn't losing anything. Then he added, "Oh, and Happy Anniversary."

"What?!"

"It was our three year anniversary three days ago."

"Oh, shit, I forgot. I'm so sorry."

"Don't worry, I remembered about a week before, but then I forgot about it, too."

We both burst out laughing.

"Well, I think that's a good sign we're doing the right thing."

* * *

Later that evening I met Tim for dinner. We reminisced, cried, and laughed some more; we held hands, and vowed we'd always be connected.

Then he asked, "So, who are you going to the U2 concert with?"

I took a long sip of tea and tried to figure out how to answer that. I didn't think it was necessary for him to hear about my crazy plans with the soldier. It would only hurt him.

"Um. Somebody. A friend."

"Who?"

"Look, you don't know him."

"It's a him?"

"Yes, it's a him," I hesitated. "Look, do you want to know the truth?"

He did, so I told him everything except for the pre-meditated sex fest part. "And we've both loved U2 since we were twelve!" I emphasized, at the end.

Tim stared at me incredulously.

"So, some Green Beret guy you met on the Internet is going to fly all the way here to go see U2 with you?"

"Yes."

"You know those guys are hard core. They don't mess around. He probably has a massive God complex and thinks he's invincible and doesn't need to wear a condom and shit like that. You have to be careful." Tim grumbled. "Where is Rambo staying?"

"With me."

He issued a stern lecture on how dangerous this was. After he asked if I wanted to get myself killed for the third time, he stopped talking and played with his mashed potatoes.

"What if he expects to hook up with you? That could be a loaded situation. Do you think he's really going to sleep on the couch?"

I had never said anything about a couch. "I don't know; we'll see what happens."

"Well, it's ok, I guess, if you know what you're getting into, and you want that, but it may be hard to be platonic." His mouth twisted while he studied his plate and then looked up with a wry smile.

I felt like a criminal.

"You didn't waste any time did you?"

I reached for his hand.

"Ah, now I can see how the dominoes are all aligned, but I appreciate it that you at least let me in on it before you toppled over the first one."

I squeezed his hand. "I'm sorry. Please forgive me."

He answered with a hoarse laugh, "Of course."

There it was: out and so ugly.

As I walked home, feelings of love and guilt gave way to an unspeakable, almost unbearable dawning inside me: The hunt was going to happen! Electric tingles invaded my body, from head to toe, and glowing sensations of elation swelled in my chest like a rising, full moon. I was literally dizzy, so I sat down on a bench while the wiser parent inside me tried to reason with my inner, hyper child.

You need to calm down! Seriously. This has manic written all over it.

Advice duly noted, but life felt so intoxicatingly delicious that I chose to remain immersed in the sensations, just for a little bit.

The soldier welcomed my news.

"So again, I'm surprised, and pleasantly, I must confess! Not only because I didn't want to come up there wondering if I were complicating your life and relationships, and now that's no longer a concern, but also, because this to me affirms so many incremental changes I've noticed in you since we first started hanging out... I don't know; you seem less stressed out about past lessons learned and more relaxed and happy! What could be more thrilling and exciting than the dawn of a new friendship?!"

I tripped hard over the word "friendship," and had to rearrange and re-shape it several times before it felt ok. I told myself a myriad of things like, "Love is friendship set on fire," to chase away the sting, even though I was the very one who gave him that magical word. I wanted to have the most passionate affair in the history of mankind, the most intense, romantic, erotic, and emotionally open experience imaginable. If I hadn't openly stated and guaranteed freedom and friendship, he would've held back. This was how it was going to be. Free, no possession, in the moment.

* * *

It seemed like I'd just left my psychiatrist's couch, but now I was back on it and not doing a great job of playing down my plans. After listening to my lengthy sanity plea, he endorsed my upcoming tryst but only under the following conditions: "NO getting pregnant and NO getting hurt! You can do all the hunting and fun tying-up you want, but there's a line. And the no-pregnant part means packing condoms in your purse, your pockets, whatever and carry them with you at all times. Really."

* * *

Next, it was Otto's turn to give me advice. "Trust me; I know how to please a man."

So, I treated him to a fancy dinner in exchange for sex tips.

I got out my journal and filled four pages of what he promised to be "blow-job mind blowers." We were obnoxious, drinking, laughing, and making various cow-milking and butter-churning motions with our hands. When Otto started bobbing his head, I had to put a stop to it. For a bonus, he threw in some choice public sex locations, Kama Sutra positions, breathing techniques, and then the really XXX tips.

"You might want to go over these notes and practice a bit before you try them, so you don't come off as reading some mental recipe or something. Also, remember to practice your 'ouchies.' If something hurts, that's fine, but you can't let out whiny, stupid 'owwwy' ouches, it has to be sexy and laden with 'Give me more...'"

When Otto finished, he took a drink of vodka and grinned, obviously very pleased with himself. Now I swear, I wasn't anywhere near this vulgar before I met Otto. But, ooh, I was so ready to dazzle.

I shared a few of Otto's tips with The Soldier later that night. "He says the Chinese Gardens exhibit on the sixth floor of the Metropolitan Art Museum is an amazing, romantic place to have subtle public sex. I think he said right behind one of the statues or in the corner by the moon-viewing terrace . There's also the Egyptian Temple of Dendur on the first floor."

"Nuh-uh..." The Soldier playfully protested.

"Hm?"

"My God, what have I gotten myself into?" He said laughing.

* * *

Several days spread into a dreamlike, joyous mission of buying accessories for our affair: candles, condoms, oils, belly chains, lingerie, and multicolored bath beads shaped like hearts and dolphins. And, of course, I had my hair done.

I instructed the colorist to, "Make it red, really red."

* * *

Date: Friday, December 2nd
Fields of Research:
    The Soldier

* * *

The Soldier's plane was late and it was nearing midnight. The only other people in the small baggage claim area were a dozen or so pot-bellied drivers waiting around with signs saying "Jones," "Rodriguez," and "Larson family." With no place for me to hide, my every movement was observed as if I were an exotic zoo attraction or the live catch on their dinner menu.

So, I studied the arrivals screen; the plane is delayed. I went to the bathroom; I could only fret. I paced the hallway and ignored the staring men. I recited to myself, *I don't look like a tart wearing a wig.*

I wore the blonde wig because he'd first met me online as Raya and because I knew I'd feel too exposed if I didn't have the protection of adornment. My outfit of sweet fitting jeans, a tight, sparkly gold tank top, and a brown suede jacket was designed to be accidentally wonderful. A few hours before, I thought I looked good, but now I felt like I was in costume. With every new tick of the clock, I felt sillier.

Suddenly, a tall guy with a grin and a swagger was rapidly approaching. I covered my eyes with my hands, laughed, and turned around. This was crazy. He looked different, not as handsome. Panic set in. Then we embraced. I felt shy, and we went out, hand-in-hand, to get a car.

Was he disappointed? He didn't kiss me or sweep me into his arms as he'd hinted he would. Steady, calm down. Shock, it's just shock.

Once in the car, I didn't know what to do, so I snuggled up against him and began kissing his cheek. I spoke in Spanish because English felt too revealing. We kissed in between words, and he brushed my "hair" away and caressed my face. My skin, my lips, my body were real, but this hair rubbing against his skin, lips, and body didn't feel right. It was one thing to parade it around on camera, but now it felt stupid. I wondered if he thought it was as ridiculous as I did. I giggled too much and made little sense, but by the time we walked up the stairs to my apartment, I felt sexy, and he looked strapping.

"I want to touch your real hair." This was his first request.

I disappeared into the bathroom and attempted to un-flatten my look. Then I took a deep breath and said a little prayer. When I emerged, his face brightened.

"Hey cutie! You look wonderful!"

My loft was a perfect love den. Decorated in deep, sensual tones of red and purple, it was full of exotic furniture, hanging Moroccan lamps, ethnic rugs, and far too many pillows. The décor evoked the interior of the genie bottle from "I Dream of Jeannie." It was sexy, and I loved it. The Soldier was amazed, but oh dear, now what do I do? Drink, I reasoned. "Would you like some wine?"

We sipped the wine and kissed amongst pillows from Afghanistan, India, and Turkey. Then I spilled a glass full all over me.

"I'm clumsy."

"No, I think you're nervous."

"No, I'm not!" But my cheeks were flaming.

More wine spilled, and soon he pulled me to my feet and picked me up in one smooth motion. I wrapped my legs around him, and we kissed as he carried me to bed. The soldier made me feel light as a feather and adored.

Then the hunt ensued. Maybe I should have left it as a metaphor and met his romantic tenderness with my own, but deep down I couldn't bear so much vulnerability so soon. So, I kicked him. "You're going to have to catch me!"

In an instant, we stripped down to our underwear. We flipped around, put each other in various vice grips, laughed hysterically, and soon we were both sweating and panting.

"Water. I need water. Stop, I can't breathe… water."

"Sorry, no water for you, this is part of *la tortura*." He pinned me, but I kneed him in his washboard abs, slipped free, and ran into the kitchen. Racing after me, he tried to pry me away from the sink, but I resisted valiantly and gulped down as much water as I could. Then I refilled the glass and threw the cold water over my shoulder and into his face. Only momentarily stunned, he shook it off and growled as he hoisted me up, flung me over his shoulder, and held me there with one arm. From my upside-down vantage point, his body looked glorious!

I laughed and shrieked as he marched us back to bed, bouncing me up and down so my sternum hit his shoulder along the way. He threw me down and pounced on me. I couldn't breathe, I couldn't move, and I felt like I was going to throw up. I shut my eyes tight and silently screamed, THANK YOU GOD!

Our savage play gave way to sweetness and sex. He kissed all over my body as he whispered, "Beautiful girl… such a beautiful girl…" He drank the wine he poured over my breasts and belly. "I could do this forever."

I was awash in red. Never had I felt so revered or showered with such pleasures. He made me feel sensual, generous, and free with my body.

At one point, he hugged me and shook me around playfully. He exclaimed, "This feels like our honeymoon. After all this time, we finally meet and are together. Happy Fake Honeymoon!"

We laughed the entire night until we passed out all tangled together. Waking up with him next to me in the morning and watching him sleep made me so happy.

* * *

We met up with a friend of the soldier's for tea and scones at the Metropolitan Museum's members-only tearoom. Later, as we strolled through the Van Gogh exhibit, the friend took me aside. "You know, I think you're magic for him; I've never seen him so happy."

Later we went for the real-deal Chinatown acupuncture at Dr. Mou's where we learned how to say "boyfriend," "girlfriend," and "I love you" in Chinese. This gave Dr. Mou the notion to treat the soldier for "Strong Penis."

"I give you Strong Penis. Good. Strong. You'll like. Long time."

We snuck into a sold-out movie. We held hands, we kissed, we wandered the city, we had lots of wonderful sex, and he squeezed my cheek affectionately during our "cute" moments. He did it spontaneously, and I loved it. His eyes sparkled, and his dimpled grin undid me. I felt the tradition and authenticity in his technique, which surely came from a childhood in Sicily filled with countless old ladies pinching him.

His energy and sense of mischief beguiled me, and our chemistry was fun and full of surprises. What truly swept me up and captivated me though was the powerful sensation of forward movement I felt with him. He was sure of himself; he knew what he wanted and getting it came naturally.

There was nothing we couldn't do.

Our hotel room in Boston was the perfect den of iniquity. Chocolates and champagne were waiting for us on our canopy bed; the fire crackled, and we immediately filled the Jacuzzi tub, perfumed the water, and sunk into the bubble bath. We did things lovers do, and then we took turns washing each other's hair. I'd never been hypnotized by a man's body until I saw his. My eyes and hands never left him for the entire hour we were in the tub. When we got out, he wore these cute, little blue boxer-like underwear made out of a weird lightweight material that drove me insane.

"Yeah, we call them 'ranger panties.'"

After our bath, he banned me from wearing wigs for the rest of the trip. "Those wigs make your head look huge. It's fine to play dress up and all, but I'm not a big fan. Your hair is so soft and so amazing to touch and run my hands through. It's simple and elegant. It is so much better than those silly wigs."

"But, I HAVE to wear my red wig to the U2 concert and seduce Bono!"

"Nope, absolutely not, no more wigs."

* * *

Seahorses were our special, symbolic animal of love, so I took him to the Boston Aquarium to pay them a visit. They were delicately beautiful yet struck me as proud little creatures. Gliding next to the seahorses, on so many gauzy, iridescent wings, were the tiny sea dragons that seemed too incredible to exist. Holding hands, we silently watched thousands of jellyfish pulsating and changing colors under the lights. He brushed my hair from my face and kissed me. The warmth and the red and blue colors of the lights pressed onto my closed eyelids as we embraced. I melted into the moment.

* * *

That night, as we slurped raw oysters, he told me, "You know, you meet people, and sometimes they are really important to you. Some are your favorite for the summer, the year," he paused, "but there's no one else like you."

After the oysters came the U2 concert. We got Bono's sweat all over us. That's how close we were. It all seemed too wonderful to be real.

* * *

The next day we were back on the bus to New York. I added up the hours of the return trip and realized that was all the time we had left together. I tried to hide my grief and looked out the window, but it kept coming. I did that thing that I absolutely hate; my chin and lips started to quiver. Where was my Kali, live-in-the-moment passion, no-regrets strength? I felt like I was dying. He tried to comfort me.

"I know it's hard to think that we have to say goodbye," was one of the things he said.

I couldn't really say anything.

We came to a twenty-minute rest stop, and he asked me if I wanted to get out for a bit. When I said no, he asked if I was sure, so I took the hint and left to give him a break.

I went into the bathroom, closed myself in a stall, and wept in deep waves of gut-wrenching tears. I wanted to get it out of my system. The rest of the ride back was quiver and tear free.

We got back to my place and rushed to gather all of his things together.

The Soldier called after me. "Stop. Come here. I don't care if I miss my flight." He searched for a song to play on his computer. Once the music started, he took me into his arms and danced with me slowly as he sang the lyrics softly into my ear. "...*I only know I love you and I always will...*" His voice faltered, and he had to stop singing.

I melted into a puddle of quivering tears.

He started again but in a whisper, "If we should lose each other somewhere inside the dark, promise me you'll remember how good we are..."

Grabbing two of his bags, I sobbed, "We have to go."

As he got into the cab, he pulled me near, took something out of his pocket, and fastened it around my neck. We locked eyes, kissed, and he disappeared. I looked down to see a little, blue seahorse suspended from a delicate, silver chain.

To comfort myself, I put on a wig and climbed into my bathtub. My loss felt epic. I couldn't stop crying, but how could I take myself seriously when I was standing under the shower with a wig on my head? Or not feel ridiculous as I soaked and sobbed in the tub, surrounded by candles and cascades of faux hair? The absurdity helped deflect reality, but more than anything, as I lovingly washed and combed the wig, I felt like I had a friend to keep me company. Like "she" had been through this with me, shared the pain, and understood.

* * *

Instead of playing it cool, like I'd planned, I went into a trance-like state for days and penned an epic poem entitled, Dreaming of Ulysses and a Siren . Unfortunately, this epic work, along with other starry missives, found their way out of my journal and into The Soldier's inbox.

* * *

At the Open Center I was greeted with "So?! What happened, come on, come on tell us!"

I showed my pictures to Otto and Linda, the Directress of Wellness. Linda studied one and exclaimed, "OH MY GOD! I've never seen this before. Your energy fields are exactly alike! Something powerful is going on here. I bet the sex was great, wasn't it!"

"He is definitely hot!" Otto said, then after a moment, he added, "Say, could you get me a picture of him in those ranger panties?"

After work, Otto did an elaborate Tarot card reading for me. "Oh My God—I can't believe it, look, he could be your Fire Prince!" I was being egged on, but I knew I was in dire need of no egging. Where was Agent Thorn? I was definitely climbing into a manic zone and not thinking clearly.

* * *

The Soldier had called several times, but I picked up the phone and said things like, "I can't talk right now; I'm writing a poem." My hope lay in the thought that if I sent him my poetic-passion package before we actually spoke, fate would be won over.

When we did talk, The Soldier hopped nervously from one superficial topic to another. Immediately frozen by his tone, I kept quiet.

"So, hey, I see you've been writing about keeping our Kundalini stoked and meeting for that eggnog and stuff but, uh... I mean, I don't know if I'm ever going to see you again."

My heart and lungs were being vivisected, so I had nothing to say.

He then softened, and I listened to him talk about "us" for a long time.

"Well, it just makes me very sad." I answered.

"Why?"

"When one person stays open and wanting a deep connection with the other but the other closes off, it hurts."

"But that's exactly the opposite of what I want to happen. I want us to grow and build on what we have and stay completely open to one another, and share our lives. Who knows, we may end up together; the eggnog thing may still happen," The Soldier brightened. "Why not? We'll keep ourselves open to it."

Following that, I wrote a couple short, damage control emails. "*Oh, and that Siren poem thing, a girl just needs a muse, you know.*"

* * *

Otto assured me that fire needed air to burn, so I should just give my Fire Prince some space to rekindle. And the spark did reignite. We reunited for a long weekend, right before Christmas, in DC.

It wasn't a fairy tale. Wonderfully sweet and intimate moments welled up between us as well as excitement and fun, but it wasn't the same. He'd pull back and act like a complete ass at times only to go back to being completely loving again. Yet he was the one who kept saying, "The next time I come up, we'll do this," and, "When we are together again," as well as, "Until the next time," right after our last orgasm.

Our farewell was perfect though. We blew kisses to each other until I disappeared onto the train platform.

* * *

Date: Christmas Vacation
Field of Research:
    Family Home

* * *

After DC, I headed to the cornfields of Illinois to spend Christmas with my family. *Why not bring a couple of wigs along for fun and for the bonus joy of messing with my relatives' heads?* No one but my immediate family had seen me for ages.

Fears of a returning depression, even though my mood was high and climbing, troubled me. An undercurrent of heaviness remained. A visit home always triggered complicated emotions that pulled me down. So, I chose to armor myself and arrive in my Mongolian Warrior Princess garb: long, badass black wig, ethnic-looking, fringed-wool skirt, body-hugging black sweater, and furry, black boots with an intimidating, skull-crushing platform heel, complete with serious treads.

My name for this look came thanks to a man who saw me wearing this outfit a few days earlier. "Hey, that looks like what you wear when you go on a date with Genghis Khan!"

"Yeah. I'm on my way to meet him now. He better be nice though, or I'll kick his ass." I felt tough and impenetrable. This was my war paint. And I was so wearing it, even if I came off as crazy.

When I arrived at my sister's house, her husband opened the door and stared, dumbfounded. He stood there and blinked. "Oh MY GOD! What the hell are you dressed up like? Wow, you look like such a freak." He let me in, finally, and broke down into laughter.

"I didn't have time to do my hair, so I popped a wig on.

Can I go take a shower and wash my hair so I can take it off?"

"Oh yes, by all means, please do."

* * *

Mom and Dad had visited me during my experiment, so they knew all about the wigs. "Just ridiculous, my gripe, don't wear that thing to dinner!" Dad protested the first night, throwing his hands in the air, but gave up very quickly, mumbling, "Fine, wear a wig, what do I care."

Mom tried one on herself and looked skeptical. "Stacy, you mean you go around all day in these?" She had it on lop-sided.

"Mom, you're not giving them a chance, they're great."

"Ok, Ok, I believe you, but..."

* * *

When Dad saw I was wearing a red wig (a shorter, tamer version of Kali) at the first of several family Christmas parties, he only gave a little grimace of protest and then poured me a glass of wine with a laugh.

My sister, who is a busy executive with two kids, a husband, and a big house, was verbally neutral, but her telltale body language and frequent mini frowns translated into: *I don't get it; why do you have to be so weird?* She listened politely, albeit rigidly, as I explained the experiment, but she never came on board.

Mom's side of the family poured in the front door, and I was greeted with enthusiastic cries of, "Oh, your hair!"

"What horse pills are you taking for that?"

"Wow, it's grown so much since last year, and that color is perfect with your skin."

Ha! My own family was fooled. I let them in on the secret, and we had a merry old time with it.

At Dad's family party, the same wig mainly caused confusion. My aunt immediately cornered me. Her constant nervous laughing tic always made me nervous. She's harmless and means well, but just seeing her triggers unpleasant feelings.

"So, what have you been up to lately, Stacy? Are you working? Oh, that's right, silly me. Your mom told me you were playing around with wigs or something. How's that going?"

"Oh, it's great." Does she know I'm wearing one?

* * *

Reminding myself that this was the season of giving, I went to church with my parents to watch the Christmas pageant. My little nephew would be performing, and it would mean more than the world to Mom, so Merry Christmas. But, if I was making the good will effort, then I could damn well wear a wig.

Following my parents, I walked down the wide, center aisle and watched as all eyes turned upon me. Thankfully, the pageant started, which shifted everyone's attention towards the stage and away from me. While the pageant was very cute, I wasn't looking forward to the forced mingling afterwards.

What a miracle, I actually enjoyed myself! Every time I turned around, a hug was waiting for me accompanied by exclamations over my "beautiful" hair, and how amazing I looked. Most people hadn't seen me since way before word had gone around that I'd gained weight, lost my hair, and had been locked in a mental ward. Now people petted and admired my head up close and personal. The powerful amount of awe my appearance elicited seemed unbelievable to me.

"I saw you walking down the aisle, and I had to take a big breath; I was so taken aback. You look like a big city model."

This was not the black-sheep welcome I expected.

During this time the soldier texted me, "*Let's talk after the holidays*," and sent me an email asking that I not text him while he was in Morocco because it would cost him a fortune.

After receiving those and then a "*Merry Christmas*," text, I wrote him an email saying I couldn't stay open to him after we spent intense time together, only for him to disappear.

That got an immediate call, and he assured me that he was just busy and trying to make Christmas happen with his family, plus preparing for his trip. Yes, we were close, we had something special, we were open, he wanted us to keep building on what we have and grow together, and he'd write the moment he could…

* * *

Date: January 2006
Field of Research:
    The Soldier Finale

* * *

When I got back to the city two days into the new year, I lovingly put the soldier's picture into a frame, placed it on a shelf where I could see it, and kept a candle lit by his side in hope and vigil at all times during his absence.

He wrote me while he was gone, and we had long, sweet phone conversations the first few days he was back. Then, he disappeared for the weekend until Sunday night. He called as he drove back from... somewhere. Something suddenly felt very wrong.

"I can't do this and keep staying open unless we decide on something, something other than 'open.'"

Deep breath on the other end. "I started dating a girl after we met in D.C."

"What! You fucking did what?!" I did the math. It had to have been *right* after. And, I knew he was calling me on his drive home straight from her bed. What followed was two hours of pleading, yelling, reasoning, and how-could-you's. He kept telling me there would never be another me. He'd probably never again find anything like our chemistry together, and we were very, very special. However, what he had with her was special, too, in a very different way. At one point, we made plans to see each other the following week. Later those plans were scrapped.

"I never said I wouldn't date other people," he said. Then, "What we have is a precious orchid, but it won't grow in Fayetteville; I live with guys in barracks ..."

"So, you're calling me on your way home from fucking her. This is bleak, and there's no silver lining. I think you've lost me, forever. Once I get off this phone, God knows how I'm going to react."

"Well, fortunately, that's something you have a choice on; you can decide how you react, and maybe you can tell me tomorrow."

My choice was to smash his picture and throw my goddamned eternal hope candle across the room while I screamed bloody murder. As I paced frantically back and forth in turmoil, I cut my foot on a shard of glass; soon the floor was painted with bloody half footprints. I was too distraught to tend to it, so it kept bleeding. I tried calling him again and again, but he had turned his phone off. I pictured him sleeping, worry free, in his little army bed, and it made me livid. I emailed him.

"Even if we didn't have an established 'relationship,' couldn't you have just waited until the scent of me was off your skin and my taste from your tongue..."

Another email.

"...I want to tell you every way you hurt me, but I agree with Jesus on this one: 'Don't throw pearls at swine'..."

Then my final text message, *"You heart raped me."*

* * *

Date: Monday, January 9th
Field of Research: Book Writing While Heartbroken

* * *

I didn't sleep.

Otto talked me through the night for hours on the phone and then emailed with, *"...All of these intense negative emotions and darkness, as well as the soaring highs and creative powers are all a part of you, and that is powerfully awesome. Go out and buy the reddest apple you can find, meditate on it and put all of these forces, good and bad into it, then take a bite out of it..."*

Before I knew it, it was noon on Monday, and Agent Thorn was at my door. I hadn't seen her in over a month, but today was the official day to start writing the book, and she was right on time. She was there to assist with research and editing; more importantly, she would force me to write.

She did not indulge my tragedy for long. Her presence kept me from returning his calls, which started that morning. While we worked, we devised dark, nefarious ways to extract revenge.

""As soon as we reached a stopping point, I made Agent Thorn go with me to hunt for an apple. Even though it was bizarre, it made symbolic sense to me. I performed Otto's apple ritual, which felt deeply cathartic, and then I even managed to write.

The Soldier and I didn't die nice and neatly. It took about two more weeks of messiness—over the phone and in chat—but then it was time to move on. To other men.

* * *

Just a couple days later, I went out for a late dinner with Steve to celebrate his birthday. My pain had morphed, at least for the moment, into a defiant, fuck-you attitude. Dinner was fun, I had a decent quantity of wine and vodka, and I didn't really want to go home alone to face my inner hurricane. It was eleven forty- five. I texted the French guy, *"What are you doing at quarter of one?"*

"Meeting you of course."

I was wearing a new, cheap, copper-streaked long wig. It looked great in the dark. Earlier, as I waited at the bar for Steve to arrive, the maître d' poured himself, and then me, several shots because, "You're cute, I'm cute, and it's a full moon."

* * *

When I met the debonair Frenchman on a street corner near the restaurant, he told me I looked ravishing and that this wig was his favorite. Thankfully, tall buildings were everywhere and that kept things nice and shadowy. We were headed back to my place with a specific activity in mind, so he'd be seeing me sans wig for the first time.

When it came off, he immediately asked, "Would you like a massage?"

Mais oui, pourquoi pas?

Mon Dieu, the sex was kinky, somewhat startling and *trés bon*. My worries that I could never again have amazing sex after being with The Soldier were resoundingly put to bed. The Frenchman was happy, too.

"Ah, *ma petite Stacy*, you are what we call in French, '*un bon camionneur.' Oui*, a good truck driver, and you know, *mais oui*, how to ride and handle it."

We were hot, but not very deep.

The next morning, we had more sex, then got dressed and went to brunch. I threw on another wig because I didn't want to spend time getting ready. Over eggs, he said some weird things like, "I felt all my energy leave my body and go into yours. It was so powerful and unnerving"

"Was I awake?"

"No, you were sleeping, but every bit of me was drawn into you. It was an irresistible pull, a gravitational force."

"Wow. But why were you afraid?"

"I don't know; it was weird."

"Well, energy can't be created or destroyed, so you'll get it back. Don't worry."

Now I felt unnerved. I was in my cheap wig, eating in a quaint Italian restaurant, and I'm sure I went on from there to say stranger things myself. I was un-showered, wearing yesterday's clothes, and very aware that my wig suffered reality poorly in daylight. Suddenly, I felt hideous looking, and it all seemed so silly.

Now, I definitely didn't feel my spirit being lured into his being, but I liked him and his truck, and I thought we could be what he was seeking—partners in passion—for a while. I wanted a distraction. I sent him a steamy email telling him I was his to ravish for the time being.

He ran away.

Hmmm. Maybe it was my array of wigs, my succubus ways, or my overly predatory email. As Steve soon pointed out, "The gazelle shall not taketh down the leopard."

* * *

As Thorn and I worked on the book, she got sick of me crying, so we decided I had to adopt two kittens and jump into real dating. She insisted I find a better gene pool and abandon *Hot or Not* hell. We created a profile with *Nerve*. Our strategy: freak 'em out right away. I posted five pictures: four of me wearing wigs and one with real hair. My handle was Kali, and my tag line read, "*Who's gonna ride my wild horses?*" I wrote that I wanted to swallow the sun, took to shape shifting, and sought men who appreciated the occasional epic poem sent their way. The weaker of heart wouldn't get past my profile.

The first date was with a forty-year-old photographer. From what I saw in his posting, he looked like a more mature, yet very handsome John Cusack. He seemed interesting, but I was a little hung-up on his age as well his five-foot, ten-inch stature. Still, he had a sexy Australian accent, so I decided to give it a try.

I wore my red wig and waited for him outside a bar. I had a mental image that I used as a search tool to size up every man that came around the corner. Fifteen minutes later, a man steadfastly approached me with a smile, I was sure it couldn't be him. But he came right up to me and gave me a kiss on the cheek. He was five-seven, if, balding, chubby, ten years older than he'd claimed, and had an impossibly wide face. I kicked myself for forgetting to beware of photographers and their angle-working abilities. Instead of being a bitch, I decided to go with the more challenging option of seeing him as a sensitive, human being.

We had a lovely evening. His game plan was to woo me with generous flattery and offer himself as an emotional safe harbor, but I politely declined when he asked me up to his place for drinks.

I walked away from that with the lesson that false

advertising wasn't a smart thing. What was he thinking? He looked nothing like his picture. Of course, I wouldn't have gone out with him if he had posted an accurate picture, but come on, why suffer my disappointment in person? Then again, who am I to be the champion of WYSIWYG (what you see is what you get)? At least now I was putting all of my optional versions out there, so fair game.

My next *Nerve* interest appeared tall and dangerous. Head back and eyes closed in his profile picture, he had an extremely sexy, yet almost dead-looking expression on his face. His tan skin and thick, dark hair spoke to me of intrigue in the desert sands. According to his profile, he was a novelist, and from what I could gather, he was also completely deranged in a far too intelligent, arrogant, vulgar, yet poetic and intoxicating way.

Agent Thorn thought he was a complete idiot. "You just like him because he has the word 'hedonism' in his description. And for the love of God, you can see his butt crack! Totally disgusting."

So fine, a shot of his bare and hunky back revealed just a teeny bit too much, but I was grateful to know ahead of time it wasn't hairy. Besides, we were fated to meet. His profile caption read, "*the side-real sun,*" and I'd stated I wanted to swallow the sun. Perfect, but first I had to figure out what he meant. Nothing came up in my searches for a "side-real sun," but I did find a "sideral sun," which refers to a slightly different way of measuring the earth's revolutions around said celestial body.

Close enough. I did the math and sent him my findings: "*Sideral days. Under the counted time of my solar sky, I have, approximately, an extra three min and fifty-six seconds to swallow your sun. I love the quotient of impossibility and roundness ... love to talk with you.*" Surely, that would get him.

He responded with a long, winding communication, written in French, telling me how he could sense and understand my energy just from those few words and the look in my eyes, but alas, he also feared that our respective brains were too much for us, and in consequence, we had both become slightly crazed. Nonetheless, he divulged his true identity and invited me to visit his website, where I'd find he spent the other part of his life as a painter, based in London. He went on to predict that if we were to meet; chaos and disorder would erupt, but he wasn't one to miss such an opportunity. Ooh, me neither!

He called Sunday morning and asked me to meet him in an hour at a café in Soho.

Yikes! I had to hurry and do something with my real hair. It didn't cooperate; just laid there, defiantly flat. I discovered a pimple that had appeared overnight on the side of my nose. I tried to cover it with powder, which just made it cakey and flaky on top of red, so I tried to fix that with lotion. Then I had a back and forth dialogue about what to do in my head.

I'll put on that new, cheapy wig! It's fun, guys love it, and the hair will overshadow the pimple!

But will it freak him out?

Surely not, since I divulged my fondness for disguises in my profile, and even put pictures up of me wearing wigs.

But remember, it's daylight out there, and I've only worn this one at night.

Oh, don't worry. It's whimsical!

* * *

Chinese New Year celebrations were in full roar in Chinatown. On my way to meet him, I got stuck in a parade. Pandemonium reigned as countless dancing beasts, banging drums, screaming kids, and flying confetti overflowed the packed streets. I gave him a call and yelled, "I'm going to be late; there are too many dragons in my way!"

"I'm coming towards you and the dragons; wait there!"

Crackling with anticipation, I stood on the least crowded corner available. A ton of TNT had been added to my fantasies after reading about his well-traveled life and seeing his artwork, which was exceptional and inspired. I spotted him walking towards me, tall and handsome, but with a strange look on his face that took him too long to rearrange into a smile. Oh God. That's not the good kind of stunned!

We headed straight for the parade; meanwhile, his alarmed aspect and hesitant greeting set off my insecurity bells. So, naturally, I found myself doing my utmost to prove his worst fears right.

After I failed to keep myself from babbling ludicrosities and he failed to convince me to get on his shoulders, I stopped in my tracks. "Wait. I think I'm being weird. Do you want me to filter myself and be … um… normal, or just go with things?"

"Oh, no filter, please, I'm here because you're insane."

"Lovely!" Just shoot me now… he's serious.

We snaked our way through the colorful throngs and made it to the plaza, which happened to be near my place, where the grand fireworks display would take place.

"I think I've had my fill of all of this banging."

I agreed, so I led us to my corner diner, right there on the square. This move ranks up there with one of the worst choices of my life. The lighting had always been harsh, stark, and blinding, and I knew it wouldn't be flattering, but amidst the deafening chaos, this was the best I could do. Maybe upstairs would be better.

We climbed the stairs and stood at the top, surveying the dining room. Light, in the ugliest shade I've ever seen, bounced off the white, mirror-lined walls and the gleaming, metal tables. A quick, ill-advised glance in the mirror revealed a nuclear carrot color radiating from my head and a red nose honking out of a Geisha white face. My knees buckled. *It's just the lighting.*

We sat in the back and started to chat. Very interesting stuff, but he looked perplexed, verging on gun shy, and got very quiet.

"Am I boring you?" I asked.

"Oh no, you're not *boring* me at all. What's your book project about?"

"Well, as you can tell, obviously, this is a wig…" The non-stop glare acted like a relentless interrogator and made me blurt it out to clear the air. After a few explanatory sentences, he didn't appear impressed, but he did ease back from the edge of his seat and his tense muscles relaxed.

We went on to talk about many things, including his book and his take on *Nerve* personals. "I think *Nerve* is more about hooking up. I don't take it very seriously. I've actually only been with one woman I met on *Nerve* because we ended up dating for a while, and she was absolutely great."

Ouch. I understood what he was really saying: *I only want to hook up with you.* It made me feel terrible on a deeper level. Being a throwaway amusement does not equal great or dateable. But this man possessed stunning artistic talent, looks, wit, a sexy British accent, the highest of educations, military experience, a life full of exceptional experiences and achievements – none of which should matter if he's a jerk – but I hoisted him up on a pedestal anyway and craved love and approval from this stranger. I advised myself to just walk away and then I opened my mouth.

"Hey, do you want to see my new kittens? I live right around the corner." What the hell am I doing?

"Oh, sure."

On the way out, he took a picture of me with his camera phone. He laughed, obviously amused, and tried to show it to me, but I shut my eyes. At that moment, I figured that if I was going to skip down the wrong road, I should quit thinking, shield my feelings, and focus on having hedonistic fun.

"Do you want a massage?" The classic sexual gateway question was asked before I had a chance to locate any kittens.

"Sure."

"But first you have to take that wig off."

So I did.

When I emerged, he watched me walk towards him with mouth and eyes agape.

Oh no, this isn't good. I'm leaving!

But then he shouted, "Oh My God! You look so much bloody better without that thing on your head. You've got great hair! You look fantastic. Oh my, worlds better."

I sat down next to him, a little hurt, and said, "But I like to experiment with my looks. It's fun."

"I know and that's cool, but that is such an obvious wig. The part is atrocious; it's made of string, thread; it's like a small little seam. Humans have a scalp, don't you know." He started chuckling deeper and shook his head in disbelief, "God, if you hadn't said 'well, this is obviously a wig,' I was going to make my escape in the next moment or so, but since you were aware that I was aware that it was a wig and not thinking you were successfully fooling me then maybe you weren't so insane. Or at least a self-aware, crazy woman."

"Well, I'm not, and that's a cheap, fun one. The others are better, I swear."

"You don't need this stuff."

By the time we were done with our massages, which honestly didn't go past heavy petting, my hair was an oily mess and the sheen of Kama Sutra oil was the only makeup left on my face. He propped himself up on his elbow and looked at me,

"Oh God, you look so good now, you have no idea. Before, you looked like a raving maniac with that wig and powder on." He motioned to his nose to give me a geographic reference.

"Really, a raving maniac?"

"Yes, A total loon." He wasn't being mean, just matter of fact. "God, you scared me."

"Lovely, I'm glad you feel so free to comment."

"Now that I know you're just fucking around with the wigs, it's all cool, but …" He had an incredulous, searching expression on his face that defies description.

This critique was weird. It stung, but everything sounded so much funnier stated in his charming British accent that, for the time being, it was too absurdly hysterical to be mortifying. I thought about trying on one of the experiment wigs to see what he thought, but then I decided that was a bad idea. I'd rather not know.

When we got ready to leave, we both looked at ourselves in my full-length mirror.

He studied me intently. "You know, you're actually quite pretty, after all." He walked away, and I laughed.

"You know, you're lucky I'm not taking this personally…"

"Well, I think you're great, very cool, but the wig and powder stuff, well, I do want you to take it personally."

* * *

"Do you think I scared him off?" I asked Agent Thorn after recounting the story to her the next day.

"Oh come on, what do you think? He called you a raving lunatic, what more proof could you want?"

"That was after he found out I wasn't one, so that doesn't count."

"Stacy, I think you have lost sight of the fact of how strange you actually are from an outside perspective."

"I'm not strange. I'm just playing around; they're just wigs."

"Yeah, to me and you, but think about it! This is the

classic Internet dating nightmare. It's bad enough when you meet someone who doesn't look like their photo – you know, older, chubbier, and balder—but you're actually in disguise! Wigs, colored contacts … It's a lot to take in on a first date."

"So, I scared him off?"

"Yep."

Then I had the swell epiphany that by now my ridiculous picture had been sent to all of his friends under the subject, *"You will never believe what just happened to me…"*

Thorn agreed. "He'll dine out on that photo for the rest of his life."

Sure, very funny, but I'm tired of being the joke. Did I just spend the last two months looking like an over-powdered, wig-wearing kook?

We decided wigs were not a good idea for first dates. And I started wondering in earnest about the whole thing. I really didn't want to keep providing the world with crazy encounter anecdotes. My feelings were drooping, and pain lurked underneath the zaniness.

Wigs were fun and great attention grabbers, but they were, for the most part, failing miserably in the real life boy-girl department. And on-line dating was pretty much date by photo. So, I put up a new personal ad. This time with pictures taken that very day of the real me with my own hair, and I edited out four of the five times I used the word "passion."

I decided that if I got more *Hot or Not* date candidates, I'd send them to this profile and tell them to get back to me if they were still interested.

Now my hair was red, red, *Run Lola Run* red. I was going for Kali red, but what I got was in that realm, though definitely more in-your-face and less pretty. The stylist talked me into getting layers cut into the front of my hair, something that I had avoided at all costs, but she convinced me with, "It'll be really sexy, trust me, I'm all about angles and illusion; it'll totally change your face."

I remained skeptical, but she said the magic word, "illusion."

When I left the salon, I didn't know what to make of myself, and I felt very different as I walked through the streets. Feeling different because of a new hairdo shouldn't have surprised me at all by now, but it did. This was my hair, after all, and it usually brought me grief and frustration. Now I felt edgier and like it matched my verve.

I met a friend on the street, and he cried, "You look like a cyborg!"

I tried to explain to him that he was referring to the blonde Daryl Hannah in Blade Runner when he actually meant that red head in the Fifth Dimension.

"Whatever man, you look like a cyborg to me, but it's a good thing, it's hot."

Oh my God, I had a look. I'd finally found my hair.

* * *

Then along came another French guy via *Hot or Not*. He was very handsome, that is if he looked anything like his picture. I wrote him back saying, "*Before this goes any further, I've changed my hair and am now a red head.*" I sent him to my *Nerve* profile. (No need to mention the change involved taking off a wig.)

He reported back that he saw nothing alarming, we exchanged a few more emails and we made a date for dinner and drinks. I would NOT be wearing a wig.

"*Salut, Mademoiselle*, I'm Alex. Ah, I see, your hair is red, very nice." And he motioned me to follow him back to the red velvet couch in the back of the chic, low lit bar.

I sat down and saw right away I had a big problem: I was pretty sure that he was prettier than me. Young, tall, luscious long locks, big brown eyes, matching adorable dimples, full lips, dressed like a womanizing spy, easy charm, grandly educated with a glamorous job at the UN. In control and didn't give a damn.

He leaned over, put his elbow on his knees, clasped his hands together, and rocked back and forth slightly. "So, here we are."

I leaned in to hear him, but he looked away and focused his interest on the young waitresses. Then he sat back, contemplated my presence for a long moment. Suddenly, he destabilized me by instantly launching into debate mode. It was the stuff of UN negotiator duels, broad then arcane topics coming and going at lightning speed. I found myself fighting for the rights of organic cabbage farmers in Provence before I took my jacket off. I sat back, finished my vodka, ordered another, and assessed the situation.

Was I here to make a business deal? Was his immediate interest in waitress-watching a power play move? This wasn't a romantic welcome, and I found myself actually squirming in my seat. My thoughts went haywire: *I don't look as good as Raya, my hair is too weak, my face must be covered in white powder... STOP. I am vibrantly fabulous. Do as Otto says: just be your fabulous self.*

He kept on being an impossibly belligerent ass. But this was my first time out as the real me, and because of that, I was determined to win a second date. I didn't have wigs to blame for any fiasco. I probably wouldn't have bothered trying so hard if this guy hadn't been such a high-stake quarry that I wanted to catch and wrench out all of his desire for me. I did feel like I'd been stripped of my armor, but just the thought of sitting across from him with a wig on my head made me shudder.

I had made sure I came into this evening with some other kind of edge. During one of our email exchanges, I had sent him a carefully selected song of mine—one that French men in particular seemed to love. For days, he couldn't stop telling me how "*magnifique*" it was. That gave a better cover with him than any wig ever could. So, since I had a foothold, I felt ready to rise to his prettiness advantage. Clearly, his appreciation of my music wasn't going to be enough, so I quickly honed my plan: wit, lots of wit, no mercy, definitely no weakness, no waiting for praise, humor, sparkling irreverence, and Good Jesus, predictability would be an instant guillotine.

I won. But I had to bribe him with promises of more music.

* * *

Then a whole slew of 'em came and went: First, Stanislov, the Ukrainian highly-trained killer and professional tango dancer. At dinner, right before he told his bloody, yet extremely interesting story, he asked me about my photos on *Nerve*. "Was your hair really that red, or did you do something to the pictures?"

"Oh, it was really that red, and next week I'm going to re-red it."

"Wow. Well, now you look more like the picture of you as a blonde. That's the real you, trust me. You look strong, brave, and powerful as a blonde." He was a strong, blond man after all.

The rest of the date was something out of a bad, bad movie. "Either you're with me 100%, passionate, and madly – either forever or never – but everything for this moment. But if not, it's just like pizza: I don't want it," he explained as he pulled me across the table and kissed me, for only a brief moment though. He got a text from the Ukraine discussing smuggling plans that needed attention. Tempted by his intrigue, but no.

I met a cute 'n' geeky, young musician who actually

requested a female "*shape-shifter*" in his profile. "When I read that you actually were one, I thought to myself, well, I have to ask her out since I specifically demanded that niche quality in a woman…"

My next suitors included a tall, redheaded, and bearded painter; a quantum physicist with a beautiful head of lush, dark curls; a Spanish biogenticist with wild, blond ringlets; and a boring guy with receding brown fuzz.

Next up was a neurologist-turned-university biology professor, who, based on his online pictures, was nerdy but cute. None of the male faces in the bar matched my search image, but one man was motioning me over anyway. After mentally shrinking his forehead by lowering his receding hairline followed by tightening up his belly and adding three upward inches to his stature, I realized this was indeed my drink date. Why do men do this? I chose to be a good sport.

After I shared a bit about my wig experiment, he revealed the shocking eel studies he and his students conducted. Through experimental testing, they observed the electric eel's mating habits and sought to understand how the evolutionary winners outwitted predators.

"Female eels, of course, go for the biggest shocks, but the males with the enormous electric charges are also easy targets, so they have to be smart, too if they actually want to end up getting laid instead of eaten." Comparisons between his experiment and mine followed.

"So, is there a lot of slippery deception going on in the eel world, too?"

"Not really. The females keep the males pretty honest. It's all about the biggest and the best, and they determine what that is. It's all the same actually; the beautiful and smartly packaged women call all the shots."

"Really? So, does this make a difference in how you treat your female students?" My eyes narrowed into two suspicious slits.

"Oh, of course. The beautiful ones I look at, but the beautiful and smart ones I actually listen to. Most of my students are women. More than eighty percent." To prove this, he took out his class roster only to discover that more than half his students were men. "Oh, I guess the women really do get all my attention. Unfortunately, I can have a very real and very negative influence in their lives, since I am their professor."

"Oh, lovely, so their academic fate hinges on whether you find them attractive."

"No, not entirely, but it does affect me."

"So, women, other than the smart and beautiful ones, have no world-shaping powers?"

"Well, it's definitely a hell of a lot more difficult, and a lot less fun, I'm sure."

"I'd tell you to fuck off, ace your class, and sue you for sexual harassment when it was all said and done." The faint, yet constant upturn of his lips mocked me.

"You just proved that I'd have power over you." He made my flesh recoil.

"Fish Brains," now his name, as far as I was concerned, was all about the absoluteness of the Darwinian dance. Our electric impulses were all wrong, and our conversation devolved into a fight.

I fought against his claims that life held no higher meaning than the sum of our biological programming. Not only was there no room for moon dust in his book, but also, if you were ugly and dull, then you should please go crawl away and die.

"You're really harsh. I don't want my reality to depend on what another thinks of me. You know, I don't want to have my self-esteem crash if some bartender isn't paying attention to me. That's sad."

"Why?"

"Well, life will be difficult if I wilt every time a man

doesn't flirt with me. I don't want to depend on men for a reason to exist."

"Well, I think that's natural. That's your now, that moment you are talking with the bartender, that's your existence at that point, and you, as a human, want attention. It affects you whether you like it or not."

"No, it doesn't have to be that way; I have to invest more in myself, my life, my art, my self-love."

"Ah well, now you're talking about something different. You're talking about plants now. I was talking about animals. Plants you grow; animals are alive in the now. The bartender and you are animals… Why not have both?"

"Well, I don't care what you think of me, but I like to take something meaningful, even transcendent, from every person I meet, not just be in it for the mating ruttings."

"Why the hell do you need to do that?"

I stared at him and thought; *Look at you, you little, balding dude! Your eel voltage is weak.*

"Oh yeah, did you keep track of your ovulation during your experiment and observe what happened?"

"Um, no."

"Well, you blew it on that one; now that would have been interesting."

* * *

Everything he'd said came from his narrow, shallow world, I kept reassuring myself. It was his perspective, not mine, so I shouldn't let it shake me to the core. But I lay in bed that night and fretted. Should I hurry up and catch a high-volt mate before my shiny tackle rusts? How long before my ovulation fails to cause a primal stir? Are we more than just dumb animals?

Yes, I'm more than just my evolutionary man-catching

talents, and men are more than their wattage zap abilities. Our buttons are not all pre-determinably pressed.

Transcendence is reality for me; who cared what he thought? But what I knew about myself dismayed me. As a general and proven rule, I did wilt if a bartender didn't flirt with me. And I could be horribly shallow. I wasn't one to give a guy a chance to reveal his inner beauty if his outer goods weren't enough to get him in the door. By putting myself under the microscope of this experiment , I unwittingly forced myself to search for a cure to my attention addiction and find my true identity underneath it all. I'd made baby steps of progress, but I had more than a bit of a stretch to go before I could claim victory. I was determined to get there, but what if Fish Brains was right? What if no one could truly be self-actualized and free? Moderate to heavy existential shakiness went on for weeks.

* * *

I started going out dancing a lot. It always made me feel good and now more so with the addition of wigs. Yes, they were freaking hot, but it was so much more fun to have huge hair and locks to play with. And they just made my dance outfits. On one of these nights out with the girls, we were taking a break at the bar when an incredibly tall, dark, thick-haired, handsome man walked in. *I must meet him*, I thought. After much planning and aborted attempts, I just went up to him and said, "I'm leaving, would you like to join me?"

So off into the night we went. One of the first things I told him as we were walking down the sidewalk was, "Ok, see this hair, it's coming off."

He took it in stride, and when it happened, he smiled and offered, "Your hair is nice. It's just… just a little flat."

"Well, it's been under a sweaty wig for hours."

"That's what I mean, it's great; it's just really flat."

I didn't look my best but, he took me into his arms, kissed me and then mused, "It's not about hair anyway, now is it?"

I pulled back and laughed, "Oh, come on! You know it matters!"

He shrugged, grinned and said, "Ok, it is kind of about hair, too…"

Chapter IX
Conclusions: The Done Do

So hair matters a little bit; And evidently more to some than others.

It should be obvious by now that my hair issues are also a metaphor for my inner demons, and for some reason most of my baggage ended up on top of my head.

I first started fretting about my hair because my grandmother did. She was a woman of flamboyant tastes, which would have been over-the-top anywhere but were unheard of in these corn-country, fifty-miles-from-a-movie-theater parts. Feather boas, glitter, beaded clutch purses, pink painted eyebrows, elbow-length silk gloves, ball gowns and all sorts of strange glamour were the norm. I adored her and spent most of my childhood putting on make-up in front of her vanity and invading her closets.

She didn't weather the onset of my first awkward stage well. She was delicate enough to approach my father with an offer. He was indelicate enough to put it to me like this:

"Your grandmother will pay for your permanent. She wants you to look nice, and it pains her to see her granddaughter's hair looking like such a mess all the time. She wants you to look like a little lady and not a ragamuffin!"

I remember being terribly wounded and was convinced I wasn't pretty enough for Grandma to like me. That's just one little thing, but it was the beginning of my preoccupations.

Sorting out what I've gathered and learned from this experiment can be more tangled and messy than "Raya" after her sweaty night of dancing.

I'll start with the happy, easy stuff. I had fun. After years of Nada-like, far-too-serious thinking, and limited exposure to giddy silliness, I now have a renewed and greater appreciation for the restorative powers of mindless, frivolous folly. Going out is good. Cavorting and consuming foods and drinks with fellow humans in social settings is a bonding and cathartic pastime. The happy-go-lucky side of me burst out and blossomed during and after this experience. And for me that was a big feat.

It was freaking hard on me—emotional meltdowns, wild self esteem fluctuations, exhaustion, social anxiety, embarrassment, itchiness, and the flashing moments when I felt like I was falling off the edge of my sanity—but it was also mad fun. In sum, I looked forward to everyday, and it wasn't just the attention. It was a creation and an inclusion into something lively. I rejoined life.

Before the experiment, I felt self-conscious and not good enough or pretty enough when I was around other women. So, when we started, I didn't quite know what I would do with Agent Thorn. Surprisingly, it was great being with her from day one, and having non-stop girl talk and time was refreshing and really good for me. (Don't tell Thorn, but it actually delighted me.) The more comfortable and in-touch I became with myself, ironically through my time spent in disguise, the more at ease I was with other women.

Now, I'm happy to be a girl's girl. I have girls' nights out, I'm in an all girls book club, I go to slumber parties, and I go on girls' only trips. I'm eighty-two per cent less preoccupied with myself and, therefore, only spend eighteen percent of my time looking in mirrors and not listening; thus, I've made many more friends.

It seems absolutely preposterous to attribute all this

miracle-making to wigs, but embarking on this wackiness set my world into motion. It also gave me an anchor in a way: a tangible form of identity to present to the world. Sure, "the wig girl" wasn't the most noble title, but the project seemed to fascinate most everyone. I had a million weird stories to tell, which led to everyone recounting their own crazy tales and nights of entertaining conversations followed.

Before the experiment, my music and other writing projects were often isolated in nature and not easy to share or build a long chat around. Those things weren't really alive for others, but this living experiment was, and people were delighted to be let in on it.

In spite of page after page of navel-gazing, a good deal of my psychological and emotional infighting piped down during the course of the experiment. I had fun making fun of myself, even when I was freaking out or being disgustingly narcissistic. Absurdity has always been a great wellspring of joy for me. Plus, I did feel happy and merrily rolled along with my wacky adventures most of the time. In short, I grew as a person and had a good time doing it.

I also experienced just how remarkably powerful masks are. My disguise was my shield. If someone didn't like me, it was the wig's fault, nothing personal. That illusion of protection afforded me the chance to be more open, vulnerable, and much less self-conscious. Our very mission, this Crowning Glory experiment, gave me another layer of distance that helped me not take things so personally. I wasn't going out "for real."

The stakes weren't that high since I wasn't playing for me and for keeps. Everything—good, bad, and wretched—was ok since it was all just an experiment. And if something intimidated me, I could rally myself and think, *Stacy can't do this, but Kali can!* Or I could make Agent Thorn go first. I was present and being me, but at the same time everything had the tinge of a surreal performance. Consequently, during all of the hours and weeks out, I got to know my "truer" self, the one underneath all my angst and magic, and I ended up liking myself! So, once the fake hair came off, I was pretty damned ok with it and a lot more fond of myself.

* * *

Of course, it's not all that easy. Vibes matter. During my crises of confidence, peoples' reactions changed dramatically. I looked exactly the same, but during these moods, any manifestation of attention or one-on-one interaction always plummeted. Guys weren't nearly as interested or didn't notice me at all if I felt insecure. And when I had my first meltdown in the blazing hot subway after about the third day, I felt completely miserable and ragingly hostile inside. Thorn and I both noted that people took care to give me a wide berth and appeared to avoid eye contact at all costs. I was shocked time and again by how much people buy into what you convey. Your energy and looks are key perception shapers that obviously influence your universe as well as the world around you. The subtlest of changes make big differences, and this dance is constantly in flux. People behave strangely around what they perceive as beautiful and/or powerful.

For me, that's not the prettiest reality because it wasn't too long ago that I didn't stand a chance in hell of getting any favors or even decent treatment as a fat, depressed, bald girl. Even when I was back to "pretty," my confidence wasn't, and my presence didn't pack much oomph. But during the experiment, others somehow looked upon "my" hair as an achievement, a victory, and people praised me and blessed it. They put me up on a pedestal for a very silly reason. Then my ego would bloat, and I'd catch myself feeling like it was mine: like I did something other than throw on five pounds of someone else's hair to deserve this feeling of ordained superiority and just reverence.

Some questions that got planted in my head during the experiment continue to nag me. Is polishing up your tackle and enjoying the shiny perks a bad thing? Isn't it ok to embrace feeling sexy and spicing yourself up? I mean, why not let that oomphed-up mood and look be a part of your personality, too? But the question that trips me up and intrigues me the most is *where is the line between manipulation and expression*? The best answer I've come up with so far is *your intention*.

Regardless of what I look like, I want to become more self-actualized and to radiate confidence and self-love wherever I go, but that's a lofty goal. It is a good sign, though, that I'm not that into wigs anymore. I'll throw 'em on as an accessory or convenience, like when I don't want to wash my hair, but I'm happy to go out as myself, too.

My philosophical, emotional, and spiritual balance was badly shaken, too. I basked in the attention but was simultaneously troubled by the superficiality and even brutality of the looks game. Even my own behavior unsettled me. I could find myself amongst the worst of the shallowness offenders. I would think my painful past experiences would make me less focused on the physical, but as far as dating a man is concerned, looks still mattered.

Before it all started, I thought I'd largely be superior in all of this. I'd be the new-agey spy amongst a non-self-aware, materialistic, and devolving society. I would uncover how ridiculous and sad it was that hair and looks equated to power in our world today. Well, that high-brow ideal lasted about a minute.

Thinking about how much of a role looks play in the mating game kept me up nights. I kept replaying a particularly disturbing scene from a wild world of mammals kind of show I'd watched: A bunch of bull sea lions on gray rocks charging up to each other, throwing their heads back, and instantly ejecting a huge red throat sack in a barking face-off. The most puffed up and reddest sack won. Although, upon Googling this just now to make sure sea lions actually do this, I believe I'm combining it with the frigatebirds' scarlet throat sack mating ritual, but in any case, it haunted me.

I'd cozy up to a bar, smile at the bartender and, out of nowhere, an image of red sacks and unhinged sea lion heads would appear. That'd start me thinking about a colorful, little bird that lives in the jungle. The males spend ninety percent of their lives rehearsing an intricate seduction dance, complete with them giving their outstretched legs teasing little strokes with their feathered wings and other hot stripper tricks, all in the hopes of winning a girl bird's heart. But sadly, most of them never get laid. And here I was with my well-rehearsed charms and my wig/big, hairy throat sack. And it worked—how fucking depressing.

I hold onto higher meaning, but I still don't know how to be ok with my place in the animal kingdom and keep the peace within my spiritual world.

My lust drive went from zero to a billion in no time, and my hunger to explore my sexuality and leap into an unbridled adventure raged. I also became fascinated and more open to all kinds of human behavior. This translated into my style and manner. All of my friends noticed a change, and most thought it was about time I upped my octane.

Even my lovely Brazilian housecleaner approved. She was busy organizing my underwear when she yelled, "Stacy, what happened? You're dressing sexy now! Good, good, much better! You're young!"

Then my sexy Aussie friend and music collaborator commented, "God, you've changed. You went from hippie chick to burlesque gypsy. God, you look like you're ready to GO. Even in the way you carry yourself—you're distracting me!"

During and since the experiment, I've been looking more at why I needed to feel suited for battle just to go on a date. I learned more about my complicated relationship with men, and the power plays I tend to engage in. My need to have a trump card over men to feel safe and in control was strong. Having an edge and hiding behind shields protected me from my deep fears of rejection and not being good enough. It often felt like I had to offer more than just who I was. These feelings and patterns go way back and have deep roots in my childhood.

I also saw to what great degree I use parts of my personality as my social shelter. My insecurity and need to fit in have developed into a great ability to read other people and complement their personalities. I find out what makes them tick, and then I adjust accordingly. It's not really a fake thing; it's more a souped-up and honed-in version of the side of me I want to show.

During the two hundred plus hours of field time, I had plenty of interactions with different people and watched myself do all of this morphing and shifting. I'd size up a situation quickly and pick out what special combo of ingredients was called for and then season myself to taste as needed. Maybe witty and edgy were essential one minute followed by a more intricate mix of, say, philosophical artist and sexed-up sailor talk.

This surprised me and could get very old. For example, I was all about sex talk and being the funny-yet-world-wizened girl with Steve. I was super-charged and unstoppable. This got tiring, but it felt expected of me, and he did seem to get bored if I wasn't "on."

I don't know if this is a great ability to relate to others or something fucked up. Everyone has different chemistry and vibes with different people, but the more confident and comfortable I am with myself, the less I find myself strategizing. I also got really sick of studying myself during all that time, and now, after writing about everything that is me for more than two years, I am thoroughly over said subject. So on the plus side: I don't bother with any of it nearly as much.

I reentered the dating world—that ne'er to be repeated epoch Thorn and I refer to as "the perfect storm." The gale had been brewing for a while, but it was unleashed by spending six weeks cavorting around the city just begging for attention and trouble and then leaving my safe yet not sexy, three-year-long relationship and hermit lifestyle self. And as I went along, trying on my various alter egos in this wacky and surreal world, I kept getting wound up higher and higher and ended up a little nuts, way over-sexed, and given to fantastic flights of fantasy. (Thankfully, I didn't go over the edge.)

I walked around feeling like a predatory feline with erotic fire in my sinews most of the time. I got into bikini waxes, sexy clothes, and steamy lingerie. Now, I didn't just want to fantasize about sex; I wanted to have it. And I think that's one of the keys to understanding my extreme reactions. The dam that contained all of the fantasizing I'd been doing for the last six years had been breached. No boyfriend was in my way, and I now had enough confidence and felt physically desirable enough to make my longings real. This possibility felt terribly awesome and filled me with almost unbearable energy. But also in the mix were all of my complicated and unresolved emotions.

The femme fatale and seductress part took center stage. This was exciting, but it wasn't a full picture of me. Actually, going fully into presenting myself as a passionate and wild woman helped me hide how vulnerable I felt about going into intimate relationships with men. This way, I was living for the moment with no regrets, so my heart couldn't get broken. And if a man didn't stay, it was because that's not what we'd signed on for. Even if I believed that's what I wanted at some point, it didn't turn out to be true. I got the fiery love affair that I'd asked for, and I thought I could handle it and not hold on for more, but the soldier liaison broke my heart.

I was happy to have indulged, but not again. Putting so much of my heart into something that obviously wouldn't last wasn't good for me.

I never could turn my emotions off at goodbye and move on without looking back. I came to realize that if I wanted a relationship to last, I needed to just calm down and let the rest of myself be seen, too. That took a while, but I think I've matured and mellowed. I am more at home in my own skin now. Thorn and I articulated the difference at the time by referring to "Stacy of two years ago." As in, "Stacy of two years ago would've dipped herself into glitter and joined the circus!"

This whole thing was a dating boot camp for Thorn and I. Before, I was freaked out by the very idea of going out, and that was a big reason I stayed with my boyfriend. The experiment revved me up and kicked me out there. I opened up to ideas and things I didn't even know existed before, and my confidence strengthened. My dating follies lasted about two months until I met a tall, beautiful man with the most stunning head of hair I'd ever seen. I gave it my all for a long time, but it didn't work. When I told my mom I broke up with him I moaned, "Oh but mom, he's so gorgeous and his *hair*. Oh, his hair!"

"I know. I tell you, what marvelous hair. It really is a shame."

So, I'm back to dating square one. But so much feels different.

First, I found my hair. It's red and edgy and I love it. First time ever. And I got so sick of hair that I think I just may be forever cured of my fixation. Second, I got over myself. As I came to know and like myself more, I became exhausted with my insecure vanity and antics and ended up leaving a good deal of it behind.

It's really hard to put myself back to the beginning of Crowning Glory when I thought it was all going to be about counting how many guys stared at me and gathering other funny statistics and outrageous stories. But it was an experiment after all, and it had its way with me.

* * *

P.S. The redhead won.

Crowning Glory Statistics

Red: Hours 34.5 / Looks 729 / LPH* 21.1

Black: Hours 33 / Looks 381 / LPH* 11.5

Blond: Hours 33 / Looks 410 / LPH* 12.4

Brown: Hours 32.5 / Looks 190 / LPH* 5.8

Natural: Hours 32.5 / Looks 218 / LPH* 6.7

Overall: Hours 165.5 / Looks 1928 / LPH* 11.6

* Looks Per Hour

Chapter X
Epilogue:
The Source of all Mystery, Religion, and Lore

The day after the experiment ended, I wore the Kali wig out just for the fun of it. Momentum was key, so I plunged into transcribing spy notes and camped out for the evening in the back of Starbucks. Not long after I'd started working on my laptop, the man seated next to me leaned over and tapped me on the shoulder.

I'd seen him here dozens of times before and during the experiment. He was always sitting in the back hunched over his computer, sketching frantically in notebooks, and lost in his own world. He had wild, long, grey hair ala Gandalf, but wavier and more freaked out, with a manic, silver goatee to match. His wardrobe never varied: black velvet blazer, black shirt, black leather biker pants, black belt with an enormous pewter buckle, and old, weathered black biker boots—all in all, a ruggedly handsome, giant of a man, but a completely disheveled one. He reminded me of a Scottish Highlands warrior who had long ago gone mad. This was the first time he'd given any sign of noticing me.

Now he smiled and confidently told me, "It is no coincidence that you sat next to me, you know?"

"Not really, why?"

"Because you are THE One." He looked me up and down seriously, studying and appraising before he gazed up at my face with awe. "Yes you are, because you have the gene. You and your tribe, the true redheads, are the primal race. The source of all myth, meaning, and mystery in the universe."

"I see. Wow." I smiled and nodded my head, encouraging him to tell me more.

"I'm writing the most important book ever written in the history of mankind. One that will change life as we know it. It will PROVE that the tribe of the TRUE redheads, *your tribe*," he paused to stare deeply into my eyes and nod in agreement at what he saw before he continued, "are the ones that carry THE gene and are the just and righteous inheritors of the keys to the cosmos."

He insistently explained his theory while showing me dozens of star constellation diagrams, astrological charts, Egyptian hieroglyphics, and mathematical formulas. He flipped through other screens on his laptop before stopping on a painting of a beautiful, medieval maiden with long, flowing, auburn hair knighting a kneeling, young man in a suit of armor with her sword. He looked at me and then pointed to the woman in the picture.

With all sincerity and longing he asked, "Don't you want to be able to do that?"

"No, that's ok." I laughed.

Disappointment washed over his face and he shook his head sadly.

"You're losing your history, man."

I smirked at him, and he shook his head again, but deeper and more sorrowfully this time.

"You're too young, of course you've forgotten. Your redheaded, white ancestors were attacked by the dark ages, and *they* stole your race's knowledge and magic. You don't remember that you are Gods."

At this time, people at the tables nearby were shifting in their seats and staring at me coldly for inciting and encouraging insanity to pontificate so loudly. I didn't care, I was fascinated and had to know more in the name of social science. Really, what are the chances that the most powerful tome ever—the one that would give redheads back their divinity—was being compiled under our noses all the while Thorn and I were doing our own research?

I pretended to go back to my work, but I was actually listening and typing as hard and as fast as I could to get down as much of his monologue as possible, which compared to the amount he was saying, wasn't a lot. Words flew and sputtered from his lips at an alarming rate.

"Do you know what Adam means? His name means 'Red.' Guess what my clan name is? 'Red.' You know, Cortez was a redhead, but he didn't have the correct gene." Suddenly he stopped and looked at me. "Is your hair truly red?"

Maybe I winced, but I managed to keep calm. I'd indulged in this for far too long.

He wasn't stable enough to be played with any longer. "Well, it's not one-hundred-percent real." I didn't dare tell him it was wig, lest he see that as proof of a hostile, anti-redhead gene conspiracy designed to stop him from finishing his book. The consequences of that misunderstanding wouldn't have been pretty.

Yet, instead of being upset at the hair color confession, he looked me in the eye and smiled knowingly. He nodded his head slowly and put his arm on my shoulder in a friendly gesture.

"Your mother is a true redhead (she is actually), and I know you still have the gene. I can tell by your energy, and the gene is recessive. Yes, you have the gene. You are a chosen one." His blue eyes, shining with the sure fire of madness, kept staring into mine. He then glanced longingly back at the red haired maiden glowing on his computer screen and beseeched his heart to her and then to me.

"Are you sure you don't want to knight me?"

Afterword

It has been almost ten years since my Crowning Glory experiment. Now that I have the advantage of looking back, I can say the experiment was a pivotal turning point in my life. This crazy experiment initiated a profound healing journey through which I was able to finally put my bouts with real-life insanity behind me.

I spent six years writing, almost daily, with Agent Thorn. This steadfast schedule and consistent creative activity did wonders to steady my soul and boost my confidence. As a result, my addiction to attention and obsession with hair (and looks in general) gradually faded away.

Today, I read this tale of my experience at that time in my life with great tenderness and compassion. The younger me was very brave, and I thank her for leading me on this life saving odyssey.

For more pictures from the Crowning Glory
experiment and for more information please go to
www.crowningglorybook.com
and sign up to hear more from Stacy Harshman.

Made in the USA
Middletown, DE
25 June 2016